How Corporate and Municipal Debt Is Rated

HOW CORPORATE AND
MUNICIPAL DEBT IS RATED
An Inside Look at Standard & Poor's Rating System

HUGH C. SHERWOOD

A Wiley-Interscience Publication

JOHN WILEY & SONS, New York • London • Sydney • Toronto

Copyright © 1976 by John Wiley & Sons, Inc.

All rights reserved. Published simultaneously in Canada.

No part of this book may be reproduced by any means, nor transmitted, nor translated into a machine language without the written permission of the publisher.

Library of Congress Cataloging in Publication Data:

Sherwood, Hugh C
   How corporate and municipal debt is rated.

   "A Wiley-Interscience publication."
   Includes index.
   1. Standard and Poor's Corporation. 2. Investment analysis. I. Title.
HG4910.S45   332.6'7   76-12099
ISBN 0-471-78585-7

Printed in the United States of America

10 9 8 7 6 5 4 3 2 1

Preface

This book is an in-depth report on how Standard & Poor's Corporation rates municipal bonds, corporate bonds and notes, corporate commercial paper, corporate leases, and other debt securities, as well as corporate preferred stock. Although many books have been published on investment analysis, to the best of my knowledge this is the first one to describe how a single investment advisory organization rates virtually all kinds of debt securities.

As you may know, Standard & Poor's is one of three organizations in this country that make such ratings. The other two are Moody's Investor Service, Inc. and Fitch Investors Service, Inc. Because of the importance of their work to the nation's debt markets, all three have acquired the status of quasi-public organizations. Of the three, Standard & Poor's and Moody's are considered the most important. Their ratings are more widely publicized, referred to, and depended on.

Although this book is not about Standard & Poor's as such, perhaps it is well to say just a few words about the corporation. It and its predecessor companies have been in business for more than 115 years. For many of these years it was an independent, publicly held company. But in 1966, it was purchased by McGraw-Hill, Inc., one of the world's largest publishers of books, magazines, and other business materials. Today it is a wholly owned subsidiary of McGraw-Hill and is independent of any other institution.

In its own right Standard & Poor's is also a major publisher. It purveys a wealth of financial information and advisory opinions on debt and other securities issued by corporations, states, cities, local units of government, hospitals, and various public authorities. All told, it currently has outstanding ratings on the securities of many thousand such entities.

Within the past two years, it has begun to rate debt securities issued by United States corporations in the Euro-bond and other foreign markets, as well as comparable securities issued by both foreign governments and corporations in this country's markets. Because there are no comparable rating organizations overseas, its opinions carry considerable weight in foreign lands.

Standard & Poor's publishes its findings and recommendations in more than 30 of its own publications, ranging from *The Outlook* to *The Fixed Income Investor*. This information is further publicized by wire services, newspapers, magazines, and advertisements.

This book is aimed at a tremendously varied audience. Although I have employed many technical terms in use in the financial community, I have tried to keep such terms to a minimum and to explain their meaning in all cases in which it does not seem immediately clear.

Among other people, the audience for this book includes vice presidents of finance, controllers, treasurers, and other important corporate financial officers. Indeed, I was interested to learn from one of Standard & Poor's executives that many financial executives do not have as clear an understanding as they might of how the investment advisory organization makes its ratings.

The book should also interest chairmen, presidents, and other executives who have an important say about the fortunes of their companies. This is partly because these executives are themselves assessed by Standard & Poor's analysts. And it's partly because the demand for capital is so great in this country that the rating a company's bonds are given may significantly affect both their cost and marketability and, in fact, the firm's overall investment quality.

The audience also includes controllers and other financial officials in state, city, and local units of government, as well as those connected

Preface

with various public authorities. Partly because of the recent and ongoing financial crisis in New York City and State—a crisis that has threatened to spill over into other areas of the country—these officials have or should have a strong interest in knowing how their securities are or will be rated. Furthermore, there is considerable evidence that many of these issuers of debt do a much less sophisticated job of presenting themselves to Standard & Poor's than do a majority of corporations.

Leading officials of foreign governments and corporations should also find the book of use. Foreign borrowings in this nation's debt markets have increased markedly in the last two years and, for a variety of reasons, may increase even more in the future.

Fourth—but not necessarily last—come students at various schools of business administration. Indeed, interest in the book may well extend downward to the undergraduate level and on out to anyone interested in a business career or in the workings of one important facet of the business world.

Many readers may be tempted to read only that chapter pertaining to the kind of bonds their organization issues. But to get the most out of the book, I believe they will be well advised to also read the first three chapters and the last. Most readers from the business world, in fact, will do well to read the fourth chapter as well, which deals with how industrial bonds are rated, even if they should be employed by, say, a bank or other nonindustrial company. It goes into great depth on certain basic matters pertaining to bond ratings.

In writing this book, I have devoted at least a few paragraphs, and usually many pages, to almost every kind of debt security that Standard & Poor's rates, with one notable exception: real estate investment trusts or REITS, as they are popularly known. I have not discussed REITs at the suggestion of Standard & Poor's itself. The fact is, the investment advisory organization has rated the debt securities of only a handful of these trusts. Furthermore, many of the trusts are either in a state of bankruptcy or very close to it. As a result, it seems likely that many years will elapse before such trusts will be able to enter debt markets in any sizable number.

I have three concluding comments.

First, in researching this book it quickly became apparent to me that the rating of bonds and other debt securities is a very complex business.

Further research only reinforced this impression, which seems true both in general and as it applies to the ratings of particular kinds of debt securities.

Outsiders sometimes opine that an issuing organization's financial data—its assets to debt ratio, for example—are all-important to the rating given its debt securities. To be sure, such data are important, sometimes very important. Yet they are rarely all-important.

In making its ratings, Standard & Poor's studies a host of factors. In the case of corporations these factors include the type of industry a company is in, its position within that industry, its management, and many, many other matters. In the case of states, cities, and other issuers of municipal bonds, the investment advisory organization studies population levels, income levels, industrial growth, and many other matters, including management.

Second, this book is not, and is not intended to be, either an attack on or a defense of the way Standard & Poor's makes its ratings. It is true that its ratings are occasionally controversial, at least within the investment community. It is also true that both it and its competitors have come under criticism from time to time, often on the grounds that they have not made sufficiently plain what factors they consider in rating debt securities—and how they assess these factors.

In a very limited sense, therefore, the book could be considered a defense, or at least an explanation, of Standard & Poor's methods. But basically it is merely an explanation and exposition of these methods —no more and no less.

Third, in researching and writing this book, I have gone to great lengths to make it as accurate as possible. Thus I have read many of Standard & Poor's internal memos and other data and interviewed nearly a score of its executives and analysts, often at great length. Also, I have allowed at least one executive or analyst to review each chapter for factual accuracy. In most cases, in fact, the various chapters were reviewed by two or more people. Nonetheless, at no time did I offer to let the analysts revise the book. Nor did they nor Standard & Poor's itself seek to make such revisions. From start to finish the book has remained under my editorial control. Such changes as were suggested and accepted were made only in the interest of greater accuracy or clarity.

I wish to express my gratitude to Brenton W. Harries, president of Standard & Poor's, for making it possible for me to interview his personnel at such length. I was known to Mr. Harries only by reputation.

Preface   ix

I also wish to thank Donald A. Moser, Standard & Poor's public relations director, and Signe Haugen, his assistant, for expediting the presentation of the idea for this book, for providing me with a wealth of written background material on the subject matter, and for arranging virtually every interview I conducted. Their work was always swift, their cooperation extensive.

In addition, I wish to thank John K. Pfeiffer, vice president of the company's bond division, for his help at a very busy time. This appreciation must be extended in at least equal measure to Hyman C. Grossman and Richard E. Huff, both vice presidents in the municipal bond department, and Robert L. Margolies, an associate manager in the same.

The list of acknowledgements pertaining to Standard & Poor's corporate finance department is lengthier. It includes Leo C. O'Neill, vice president in charge of the department; Kenneth M. Alterman, Juliette L. Gould, Norman Johnson, and Roy P. Weinberger, all department managers; Thomas G. Fendrich, an associate manager; Dominick G. Di Palma, department consultant; Edward C. Bray, assistant to the vice president; and Jerome C. Corcoran, James J. O'Meara, Jane S. Peck, and Michael J. Seaman, all analysts. I also wish to thank Rosemary De Luca, the receptionist on Standard & Poor's 15th floor, for her frequent assistance.

This book has not been easy to research or write. But I have found the work interesting, informative, and useful. I hope you do so, too.

HUGH C. SHERWOOD

White Plains, New York
March 1976

Contents

1. The Debt Economy, 1
2. What Standard & Poor's Ratings Signify, 9
3. The Mechanics of Rating Debt Securities, 21
4. How Industrial Bonds Are Rated, 27
5. How Other Corporate Financing Vehicles Are Rated, 39
6. How Utility Bonds Are Rated, 47
7. How Railroad and Airline Bonds Are Rated, 35
8. How Bank Holding Bonds Are Rated, 65
9. How Finance Bonds Are Rated, 79
10. How Insurance Bonds Are Rated, 89
11. How Foreign Bonds Are Rated, 99
12. How Commercial Paper Is Rated, 109
13. How Municipal Bonds Are Rated, 115
14. How to Get a Better Rating for Your Bonds, 137
    Appendix, 145
    Index, 159

How Corporate and
Municipal Debt Is Rated

The Debt Economy 1

In this, our Bicentennial Year, the dawn of our third century as a nation, much will be said about the spiritual, moral, legal, artistic, and scientific debts we owe our forefathers. Yet, aside from the continuing furor over New York City's ongoing financial crisis, probably relatively little will be said about the financial debt we owe ourselves.

Yet the amount of this debt is staggering. And much of its growth has occurred during our own lifetimes, in the 30 years that have elapsed since the end of World War II.

At the beginning of 1946, the United States Government owed nearly $260 billion. The nation's states, cities, and other municipal borrowers owed about $15 billion, and its corporations owed some $25 billion.

Today the federal Government owes some $566 billion. Municipal borrowers owe an estimated $223 billion, and corporations owe about $298 billion.

This represents, overall, a better than threefold increase in debt in just three decades. What's more, these figures do not include consumer and certain other kinds of debt, which have also grown by leaps and bounds.

Indeed, so great has been the growth in all kinds of debt that in 1974 *Business Week* characterized America as a debt economy without peer. This nation, said the magazine, "has the biggest lenders, the biggest borrowers, the most sophisticated financial system. The numbers are so vast that they simply numb the mind."

Not only has the amount of debt increased, so has the rate at which it has increased. One study indicates that the average annual increase was 4 percent between 1929 and 1947, 6 percent between 1947 and 1965, and 9 percent between 1965 and 1974.

Why has all this come about?

One reason is that consumers have demanded more and more of both the necessities and the good things in life. To increase production to meet these demands, corporations have had to borrow at an ever-accelerating rate.

Another reason lies in a vast increase in spending by the federal government, which has not only stepped up welfare and similar payments at a tremendous rate but, in an effort to stabilize the economy, also has usually operated at a deficit. This, too, has necessitated heavy borrowing.

In recent years, however, inflation has been the most important cause of the increase in debt, especially in the corporate area. Corporations have not been able to generate enough money through depreciation to meet the cost of replacing whatever they are depreciating. As a result, they have had to finance more and more of their capital spending externally. Because they have been able to raise only a fraction of what they need in the stock market, they have had to borrow in the debt market.

A decade ago, *Business Week* reports, American business borrowed 60 cents for each $1 it raised internally. By 1974 the first of these figures had risen to $1.60.

Along with a tremendous increase in the amount of debt outstanding has come a spectacular increase in the rates of interest that must be paid on this debt. As Henry Kaufman, the internationally known economist who is a partner in Salomon Brothers, a leading investment banking firm points out: "The post-World-War-II rise in interest rates began gradually and then, during the past 10 years, accelerated with awesome momentum. Thus the rates on prime, seasoned, long-term corporate bonds were around 2.5 percent in 1946. They then moved up irregularly to about 5.5 percent by 1966. But by 1974, they had skyrocketed to 9.5 percent. And, of course, the rates on new high-grade corporate bonds soared to even loftier heights. This powerful upward swing in the cost of money has dwarfed all others in American history."

The Debt Economy

Nor have corporations been the only ones affected. Municipal bond issuers have also had to pay higher rates of interest. Here, too, inflation is probably the major cause. New York City's financial crisis has also played a role, however, because it has shaken the confidence of investors. As a result, they are demanding greater rewards for the risks they incur by investing in municipal bonds.

Is this whole situation cause for concern? Of course, it is.

A decade ago, *Business Week* reports, American business had nearly $4 of equity (stock) for every $1 of debt. Today, the magazine reports, the first figure is nearer $2 and still plunging. In addition, the magazine says, a decade ago, business earned about $5 for every $1 it owed in interest on its debt. Today the first figure is nearer $2.

The fact is, many corporations are effectively precluded from borrowing in the long-term debt market. Their financial credibility is suspect. In order to borrow, they would have to pay astronomical rates of interest.

Many municipal borrowers are in the same boat. In their case, however, additional factors are sometimes at work. One of them is an increase in so-called moral obligation bonds. These bonds are issued by a state agency, a city agency, or a public authority and are backed by some parent organization—often a state itself. This backing, however, does not constitute a legal guarantee by the parent that payments of principal and interest will be made—and be made on time. It merely constitutes a moral obligation. As many financial experts have pointed out, a state or any other parent can always renege on a moral obligation at some point in the future.

An editorial in *The New York Times,* December 13, 1975 states: "The root of [New York] State's trouble lies in the moral obligation funding device . . . adopted by . . . the legislature in the early 1960's to avoid the constitutional requirement that state bond issues receive prior endorsement in a statewide referendum. Freed of this sobering constraint, the [Housing Finance Agency] and other newly created agencies proceeded to pile up debt at a staggering rate to construct housing, hospitals, schools, and other socially desirable—but not necessarily creditworthy—facilities.

"The result was a tripling of New York State's total debt in the last decade to more than $15 billion, a rate of increase far higher than that of New York City or any other state. . . . Today more than two-thirds of the state's long-term debt is in moral obligation bonds—not backed by the state's full faith and credit. New York is responsible for one-fourth of all such nonguaranteed debt in the nation."*

Another problem faced by municipal borrowers is that they have long provided much less information about themselves to investors than corporations have. Recently this dearth began to take its toll.

In December 1975 the City of Richmond, Virginia tried to sell a $25 million bond issue. This municipality had been coming to the long-term debt market for 20 successive Decembers, and its previous issues had been given a very high credit rating. But this time it came away empty-handed. Three prominent investment banking groups that had ordinarily bid on Richmond's bonds refused to do so. The bankers indicated that if the bonds suffered any difficulties in the marketplace, they might be sued by investors who would complain that they had not been well enough informed about the bonds' potential drawbacks. The bankers said they wanted corroboration of the completeness and veracity of Richmond's statement offering the bonds for sale before they would bid.

Municipal bond issuers face yet another problem. In 1975, in trying to avoid defaulting on some of its debt, New York City resorted to an unusual ploy. It declared a moratorium on payment of some of the principal it owed. Specifically, it gave the holders of some $1.6 billion of its notes a clear-cut choice: They could trade their notes, which were about to mature, for 10-year bonds issued by a new New York State agency known as the Municipal Assistance Corporation, or they could hold on to the notes. But if they took the latter course, they would be paid less interest than they had been receiving, and they would not get their principal back for 3 years.

Many observers believed that the moratorium was, for all practical purposes, a default. After all, a bond issuer agrees not only to pay back the principal it borrows, plus interest along the way, but also to do both of these things at specific points in time.

What was really worrisome to many, however, is that the moratorium set a precedent. It opened the door for cities and states elsewhere to delay principal and interest payments if they get into financial difficulty. For this reason it tarnished the credibility of virtually all municipal bond issuers to at least a slight degree.

---

*In March, 1976 the New York State Legislature enacted legislation that effectively prevents the state's various agencies from issuing any more moral obligation bonds except to complete the financing of projects already under way.

The Debt Economy

In view of all these problems, what is the outlook for the future? Says Henry Kaufman:

> The abuse of our economic and financial system has produced an assortment of countervailing forces that may lead us away from our recent serious troubles. What are some of these forces?
>
> There is an increasing skepticism among the people concerning the ability of government to live up to its promises. We have experienced high employment, high rates of inflation, and financial stringencies that were unthinkable a decade ago. And we have begun to realize that government cannot solve problems merely by turning on the spending spigot and that it cannot protect us from a variety of adversities that, in some instances, may have been actually aggravated by official policies.
>
> This skepticism is likely to cause business and other private sector decisions to be arrived at with an improved sense of risk and reward. It is also likely to cause increasing pressure on government to improve its efficiency and to be more realistic in setting targets.
>
> In addition, we should not overlook the powerful discipline that inflation has forced upon us. Inflation has heaped a large volume of debt on our economy. But it has also made many organizations far more circumspect in their decisions. Business strategy today places a high priority on maintaining a high credit standing. The era of excessive financial leveraging is over. It cannot return quickly. For the first time in the postwar period, an entire generation is learning the hard way the consequences of too much borrowing and other imprudent financial practices.

On top of this, Kaufman lists certain changes in government policies, in particular a tightening of its monetary policy, as a countervailing force likely to bring about a slowdown in inflation. He also cites the nation's deep commitment to democratic principles, its stable political system, and its great natural economic wealth as inherent strengths that will serve us well.

Obviously, Kaufman is sanguine that the lessons of yesterday are being learned and that we will become financially stronger in the years ahead. But what if he is wrong? Then he predicts "far greater havoc than anything that has occurred to date." The federal government and a few other borrowers with high credit ratings will dominate the debt markets. Borrowers with poor and possibly even mediocre credit ratings will be suddenly devastated. Failures will abound.

It is within the context of this total situation, with all its possibilities for good and ill, that we must now turn our attention to Standard & Poor's Corporation. As noted in this book's Preface, it is one of three organizations in this country that rate corporate and municipal long-term debt—and often short-term debt as well.

In rating debt, its purpose is brief and clear-cut. It simply endeavors to determine how likely it is that the issuer of the debt will be able to pay back the principal it borrows, plus interest, and make these payments at those times at which it has legally agreed.

The chapters ahead tell in great detail what the company's individual ratings signify, how the company goes about arriving at these ratings, and what factors it considers in doing so. Suffice it here to make three points that are very important to a basic understanding of its rating process.

The first is far and away the most significant, for it applies not only to the rating of corporate and municipal bonds, but also to the rating of all other kinds of debt and equity securities. The point is, there is no magic formula for arriving at a rating. Many quantitative and qualitative factors must be considered. In other words, deciding on a rating involves many matters of judgment, not merely an analysis of statistics.

As Brenton W. Harries, president of Standard & Poor's, puts it, in discussing corporate bonds in particular: "Rating bonds and other securities is not and never will be a precise science. There are simply too many variables. We are called upon to judge a tremendous variety and combination of businesses and, even if we were to attempt to develop a formula applicable to just one kind of business, we know from experience that exceptions would destroy the rule."

Second, Standard & Poor's judges debt securities on both an absolute and a relative basis. In other words, it judges them against an ideal in terms of the various factors it considers in making a rating. But it also judges them against securities put out by other companies in the same industry or, in the case of municipal bonds, against securities put out by other states, cities, and public authorities.

"The result," points out Roy P. Weinberger, a manager in Standard & Poor's corporate finance department, "is that the bonds of the best company in a given industry are not necessarily given our highest rating. They may receive only our third or fourth highest. Obviously, however, the bonds of other companies in the same industry will not receive higher ratings. Indeed, all or most will get lower ones."

Third, emphasizes Leo C. O'Neill, vice president of Standard & Poor's corporate finance department: "By definition, a rating agency must look at a company on the basis of how it is likely to perform under the worst

The Debt Economy

conditions, not the best. As a result, the agency must constantly search for, identify, and discuss the negatives in the debt issuer's overall situation." What is true of companies is also true, of course, of states, cities, and other borrowers.

What Standard & Poor's Ratings Signify   2

The ratings Standard & Poor's and its two competitors give to bonds and commercial paper are important both to the organizations that issue such securities and to the investors who consider buying them.

In the case of a bond, which is, of course, a long-term debt obligation that usually matures in anywhere from 5 to 40 years, a rating is designed to indicate how likely it is that the issuer will be able to meet principal and interest payments on time. In the case of commercial paper, which is a short-term debt obligation that matures in anywhere from 1 to 270 days, a rating is designed to indicate how likely it is that the issuer will be able to meet its cash needs on time.

A rating is important to a bond issuer primarily because it will have a pronounced effect on the interest the issuer will have to pay, although, to be sure, other factors, such as the size and maturity of the issue will also play a role. Yet in general, the higher the rating, the less interest potential investors will require.

For example, consider June 1975. If an industrial company had issued a bond at that time and if the bond had received Standard & Poor's highest rating (AAA), the company would probably have had to pay interest of about 8.75 percent, presuming the bond could not be refunded for at least 10 years. If, however, the bond had received Standard & Poor's third highest rating (A), the company would probably have had to pay interest of 9.75 percent.

Although this difference in interest amounts to only 1 percent (100 basis points), it must be paid each and every year the bond is outstanding. Thus, depending on the size of the issue, the difference may result in added interest costs of millions of dollars.

For example, if the company were seeking $25 million, repayable in 25 years, the extra interest alone would amount to $6.25 million over the life of the bond, assuming its principal amount remained outstanding for its full life. If the company were seeking $100 million, repayable at the end of the same period, the extra interest would total $25 million.

There is another reason why ratings are important to corporations and municipalities. If their securities receive markedly low ratings, they may not be able to issue them at all. There just won't be enough investors interested in them.

In 1970, for example, the Pennsylvania Company, the holding company for the Penn Central Railroad, wanted to issue $100 million of bonds. It was willing to pay a high rate of interest to do so. Yet shortly before the bonds were to be brought to market, Standard & Poor's gave them a relatively low rating. As a result of this and other adverse publicity, they were never actually issued.

Low ratings can have other damaging effects on a corporation or a municipality. Thus they may harm its prestige, making it more difficult to issue common stock or to borrow money from banks and other institutions.

Investors are just as interested in ratings—for the opposite reason. Some investors may be interested in bonds with relatively low ratings because the bonds will return more interest than bonds with higher ratings. The overwhelming majority of investors, however, seek bonds with relatively high ratings. They are willing to accept less interest than they would obtain from low-rated bonds in exchange for greater assurance that the principal and interest that is owed them will be paid—and paid on time.

Now, precisely what ratings does Standard & Poor's give to bonds and to commercial paper? What do these ratings signify?

Let us look at corporate bonds first. The investment advisory organization gives these securities one of 12 ratings, ranging from triple-A (AAA) through single-D (DDD). The meaning of the ratings is as follows:

What Standard & Poor's Ratings Signify

- AAA—Bonds with this rating are viewed as obligations of the highest grade. They possess the ultimate degree of protection of both principal and interest. In the marketplace their prices move up and down only as long-term interest rates move up and down. Hence they provide maximum safety on all accounts.
- AA—Bonds with this rating also qualify as obligations of high grade. In the majority of cases they differ from triple-A bonds only in small degree. Their prices also move up and down only as long-term interest rates do so.
- A—Bonds with this rating are regarded as upper-medium grade. Interest and principal are regarded as safe, and the bonds have considerable investment strength. They are not, however, entirely free from the possibly adverse effects of changes in economic and trade conditions. In the marketplace their prices predominantly reflect changes in long-term interest rates but also, to some extent, changes in economic conditions.
- BBB—Bonds with this rating are considered medium grade and fall on the borderline between definitely sound obligations and obligations in which a speculative element begins to predominate. These bonds have adequate asset coverage and are normally protected by satisfactory earnings. Yet they are susceptible to changing economic conditions, particularly depressions, and need constant watching. In the marketplace their prices are more responsive to business and trade conditions than to interest rates. These bonds are the lowest that qualify for investment by commercial banks.
- BB—Bonds with this rating are viewed as lower-medium grade and have only minor investment characteristics. In the case of utilities, interest is earned consistently but by narrow margins. In the case of other issuers, interest is earned, on average, by fair margins. In periods of economic stress, however, deficit operations are possible.
- B—Bonds with this rating are considered speculative. Payment of interest cannot be assured when difficult economic conditions prevail.
- CCC—Bonds with this rating are viewed as outright speculations. Interest is paid, but continuation of such payments is questionable in periods of poor trade conditions.
- CC—Bonds with this rating are even more speculative. Their issuers may have agreed to pay interest only if they earn income, and under any conditions payments may be small.
- C—Bonds with this rating also return interest only when their issuers earn income. In their case, no interest is being paid.

- DDD, DD and D—Bonds with these ratings are in default on payments of principal, interest, or both. The particular rating a bond receives indicates its probable salvage value in relation to other bonds' probable salvage values.

In 1974 Standard & Poor's began adding plus and minus signs to some bonds in its second through its fifth highest categories—that is, to certain bonds rated AA, A, BBB, or BB. A given bond in one of these categories, whether a new or seasoned issue, may be rated A− or BBB+ or BB−. These symbols are designed to indicate the relative credit standing of such bonds within their rating category. For example, bonds rated BBB+ are viewed as slightly safer than other bonds with triple-B ratings.

If you have studied these ratings carefully, you will have noticed that the great dividing line involves bonds rated triple-B. All bonds with higher ratings are considered relatively safe investments. All with lower ratings are considered at least slightly unsafe. Many investment counselors advise investors not to buy them unless the investors are very knowledgeable about bonds and fully aware of the risks they are taking.

What about the bonds right on the dividing line—those with triple-B ratings? Bonds with this rating are the first to contain a speculative element. As a result, some institutions refuse to invest in them. Others believe that if they exercise ordinary prudence, they can find plenty of bonds with this rating that represent good investments. In any case, these bonds are the lowest rated of those bonds known as investment-grade issues.

Surprising as it may be to you, the overwhelming majority of bonds receive good ratings. A study done in 1972 by Salomon Brothers showed that of nearly 3900 corporate bond issues (as opposed to issuers) rated by Standard & Poor's, more than 83 percent were rated AAA, AA, or A. Approximately another 10 percent were rated BBB.* Standard & Poor's recently estimated that an even higher percentage of municipal bonds carried one of its four highest ratings.

The high incidence of high ratings should not be surprising, because, in the case of corporate bonds, Standard & Poor's is not assessing a

*See *The Anatomy of the Secondary Market in Corporate Bonds,* Henry Kaufman, Salomon Brothers, New York, 1973.

What Standard & Poor's Ratings Signify

company's ability to become the leading firm in its industry or to multiply its earnings several times over within a short period of time. It is merely assessing the company's ability to pay back what it borrows, plus interest along the way, and to do both of these things on time.

Naturally, bond ratings do not necessarily remain fixed for all time. They can and sometimes do change, moving either upward or downward. In this connection Standard & Poor's reviews all its ratings at least once a year, more often if circumstances warrant. Leo C. O'Neill, vice president in charge of the company's corporate finance department, estimates that in 1974 Standard & Poor's changed its ratings on the bonds of fewer than 3 percent of all corporate issuers. In a typical year the figure for municipal bonds is not dissimilar.

Obviously, then, bond ratings do not move up and down like a yo-yo. Once a rating has been changed, for better or for worse, it is likely to remain as its new level for at least a year, until Standard & Poor's becomes convinced that relatively permanent changes have again taken place in relation to the company or municipality in question.

Everything that has been said so far applies to the rating of straight corporate bonds. There are, however, special kinds of corporate securities, such as corporate notes and convertible bonds, to which everything said thus far does not apply. The differences in rating these latter kinds of securities are explained in Chapter 5.

You should be aware that Standard & Poor's does not rate all bonds or other debt securities. For example, it does not rate any securities issued by the United States Treasury or other federal agencies that do not carry a government guarantee. The one exception involves bonds issued by the Tennessee Valley Authority. Although it is often listed as an agency of the government, it is really more of an instrumentality. Also, the principal and interest payments it makes are payable solely out of the income it obtains from its sales of power. Therefore, the authority can be analyzed as an operating entity in its own right rather than in terms of its relationship to the government.

For that matter, the investment advisory organization does not rate all corporate issues either. Thus it does not rate bonds brought out by corporations without demonstrable operating records nor bonds brought out by corporations that do not provide audited financial statements.

Let us look now at commercial paper ratings. These ratings are just as important to the buyers and sellers of such paper as are the ratings given to bonds, and for the same reasons. A rating reflects the degree of likelihood that a commercial paper issuer will be able to pay back what it borrows on schedule. It also plays a dominant role in determining how much interest the issuer will have to pay, although the reputation of the company in question, the amount of commercial paper it issues, and the frequency with which it enters the market are factors, too.

Interest rates on commercial paper can be highly volatile, and they sometimes move up or down several percentage points within only a few months. Yet, as should be obvious, there is almost always a spread between the interest that must be paid on top-rated commercial paper and paper rated even one notch lower.

Standard & Poor's issues one of six ratings to commercial paper. These ratings are A-1, A-2, A-3, B, C, and D. In actual practice, however, it issues only one of the top three ratings, because commercial paper issuers refuse to accept any that are lower. Since 1969, when Standard & Poor's began rating commercial paper, there simply has been no market for paper rated B or lower. Companies that learn from their dealers or other sources that their paper would probably be rated that low do not bother to come to Standard & Poor's, nor do they try to enter the national market.

What do the ratings signify? For a company to receive one of the three ratings within the A category, it must meet the following six criteria:

1. Its liquidity ratios must be sufficient to meet its cash requirements. In the case of industrial companies these ratios include the acid test ratio, the current ratio, the cash flow to current liabilities ratio, and the cash flow to long-term debt ratio.

The acid test ratio relates the issuer's cash, cash equivalents, and accounts receivable to its liabilities. What constitutes an adequate ratio varies markedly from industry to industry. That's partly because some industries carry very large amounts of inventory and receivables, some very small ones. As a result, Standard & Poor's compares how the company in question stacks up against other companies in the same industry.

The current ratio relates current assets to current liabilities. In most cases Standard & Poor's prefers that current assets exceed current liabilities by at least two to one. In 1974 and 1975, however, many firms' current ratios slipped below this level, and because of strong inflationary pressures, this trend may continue.

What Standard & Poor's Ratings Signify

The next ratio relates cash flow to current liabilities. Standard & Poor's likes to see cash flow equal to 40 percent or more of current liabilities and ordinarily regards 30 percent as the minimum for an A rating.

The final ratio relates cash flow to long-term debt. Essentially the same criteria apply as in the case of the preceding ratio.

It cannot be stressed too strongly, however, that in the case of all of these ratios the guideline numbers are not applied absolutely, by any stretch of the imagination. The nature of the industry a company is in, its operating record, its capital structure, and the composition of its cash flow frequently cause the investment advisory organization to accept more or less than the ideal.

In the case of certain other kinds of companies, such as utilities and finance companies, Standard & Poor's studies other, somewhat different, liquidity ratios. For example, in assaying utilities, the rating agency checks current liabilities as a percentage of revenues, cash flow as a percentage of current liabilities, and short-term debt as a percentage of capitalization.

2. If the issuer has long-term senior debt outstanding, this debt should carry a rating of single-A or better. Occasionally firms whose long-term debt is rated only triple-B can issue paper that qualifies for an A rating, but to do so, their short-term outlooks must be very good.

3. The issuer must have access to at least two additional sources of funds. These sources may include the public bond market, the private bond market, one or more banks, or other outlets.

4. Both the issuer's earnings and its cash flow must be in an upward trend. Exceptions are occasionally made if the issuer faces unusual circumstances.

5. Typically the issuer must be in a well-established industry, and it must hold a strong position therein.

6. The reliability and quality of its management must be unquestioned.

How is commercial paper that qualifies for a rating in the A category further broken down? Standard & Poor's has not devised any formal definitions of its A-1, A-2, and A-3 ratings. The exact rating a given issue receives depends on the relative strength or weakness of the issuer in relation to the above criteria.

Leo O'Neill, vice president of corporate finance, adds this interpretive commentary:

A company whose commercial paper receives an A-1 rating is one whose financial strength and liquidity are overwhelming. It is a General Motors Acceptance Corporation, a Sears, Roebuck, a Shell Oil, or a Union Carbide.

A company whose paper is rated A-2 usually has an excellent operating record and strong liquidity. And it exhibits no basic weaknesses.

A company whose paper is rated A-3 represents a good credit risk, but usually has one basic weakness. For example, it may be growing too rapidly and be constantly in need of capital. Or it may have a temporary earnings problem.

As we have seen, no company has ever accepted a B rating. Yet Standard & Poor's does not expect that this will always be the case. Thus we had better glance at the criteria for such a rating. There are five of them. The issuer's liquidity ratios must be good, although not necessarily as good as those of companies whose paper receives one of the A ratings. Its long-term debt must be rated double-B or higher. Although its earnings record may be unimpressive—perhaps because the company is not yet fully developed—it must have demonstrated earning power. It must also have access to at least one other source of funds, and the reliability and quality of its management must be at least average.

The C rating is reserved for companies that are in financial difficulties. For example, there may be doubt as to whether the companies can maintain a satisfactory level of earnings. The D rating would be used for companies that are in or headed for default.

One other question is of interest: If a company receives a high rating for its long-term bonds, is it also apt to receive a high rating for its commercial paper? In general, there is a close relation between ratings on long-term bonds and commercial paper, but the relation is not absolute and does not always prevail. Says Brenton W. Harries, president of Standard & Poor's:

The use of a long-term bond rating to assess commercial paper can be dangerously misleading. Good corporations, like good people, can be temporarily embarrassed.

The liquidity of a corporation with commercial paper outstanding faces a more stringent test of timing than does the liquidity of a corporation with bonds outstanding. By definition commercial paper may not be outstanding longer than 270 days. Therefore, provisions for repayment must be made virtually as the paper is being sold. Planning for the payment of interest and eventual retirement of a bond issue may be much more leisurely, removing the pressure of time somewhat from the test for a rating.

Let us look now at how Standard & Poor's rates municipal bonds.

What Standard & Poor's Ratings Signify

These bonds fall into two broad categories: general obligation bonds and revenue bonds. General obligation bonds are usually secured by all of the financial and other resources available to the state or city that issues them. Revenue bonds, on the other hand, are usually secured only by specific revenues, such as gasoline taxes or highway tolls. Standard & Poor's takes account of the difference in security behind general obligation and revenue bonds.

With five exceptions, Standard & Poor's uses the very same symbols to rate both kinds of municipal bonds as it does to rate corporate bonds. The exceptions involve the letter symbols CCC, CC, C, DDD, and DD. The investment advisory organization does not use these symbols to rate municipal bonds, because, simply, there is no need to do so. Virtually all municipal bonds are rated triple-B or higher. The few that are not are easily categorized as double- or single-B bonds or as in default.

Now how do the symbols it does use apply to general obligation bonds?

- AAA—This symbol is applied only to bonds of the highest quality. The issuers of these bonds are in the best position to make principal and interest payments on time. Furthermore, they enjoy superior management, have only a moderate amount of debt outstanding, boast a revenue structure that seems more than adequate to meet future spending needs, and are apt to suffer only small declines in income during periods of economic stress.
- AA—This symbol is applied to bonds of very high quality. Their issuers enjoy all the advantages that issuers of AAA bonds do, but to a slightly less pronounced degree.
- A—This symbol is used to designate bonds of good quality. Their issuers are believed to be fully capable of making principal and interest payments on time, but they suffer from some one weakness that could impair this ability under adverse circumstances. For example, their local economies may not be as strong as those of other issuers, or they may have a greater amount of debt outstanding, or the balance between their revenues and expenditures may be slimmer, or their managements may be of less than top-flight quality.
- BBB—This symbol is given to bonds that are viewed as of medium quality. Principal and interest payments are ordinarily considered relatively safe, but the issuers of such bonds have their weaknesses. Indeed, the chief difference between issuers of A and BBB bonds is that the latter suffer from some one weakness like those just cited to a

very substantial degree or from two or more such weaknesses. Under certain circumstances, this could impair their ability to pay off their debt or the interest thereon on schedule.
- BB—Bonds with this rating are viewed as speculative. They enjoy some of the strengths of the bonds cited, but these strengths do not predominate; instead, weaknesses do. As a result, the bonds are not ordinarily considered suitable investments for prudent institutional and individual investors.
- B—A bond given this rating is considered low grade. It enjoys virtually none of the strengths cited earlier. Indeed, it may be approaching default on either principal or interest payments.
- D—Bonds that carry this rating are in default on payments of principal, interest, or both.

When applied to revenue bonds, these symbols have similar, but not always identical, meanings. Let us see:
- AAA—Revenue bonds with this rating are of the highest quality. The basic security provisions governing the bonds—for example, the level of earnings that must be achieved or maintained before additional bonds can be issued—are rigorous. The issuers' ability to make principal and interest payments on time has been and seems likely to remain substantial, and the revenues that have been pledged toward such payments are exceptionally strong. In addition, the issuers enjoy superior management.
- AA—Revenue bonds that carry this rating are considered high grade. They differ from triple-A bonds only in slight degree.
- A—Revenue bonds with this rating are of good grade. Yet all along the line they differ in some degree from bonds with the two highest ratings. Thus their basic security provisions are satisfactory but less stringent. Their ability to make principal and interest payments on time is good but not exceptional. The revenues they have pledged toward such payments are stable but could become somewhat erratic under certain circumstances, such as increased competition, and their managements appear merely adequate.
- BBB—These bonds are considered medium grade. Basic security provisions are merely adequate. Ability to make debt payments is only fair. The revenues pledged toward these payments could vary substantially, and management could be stronger.

What Standard & Poor's Ratings Signify

As for the three lowest ratings, the same comments that apply to general obligation bonds apply to revenue bonds. Thus investment characteristics no longer predominate among bonds rated BB and are virtually nonexistent among bonds rated B. Issues rated D, of course, are in default.

Like corporate bonds, both kinds of municipal bonds sometimes carry a plus or minus sign in addition to a letter symbol. These signs are applied only to bonds in the categories ranging from AA through BB. A plus sign indicates that a bond is slightly superior to others in its category but not sufficiently superior to warrant a higher rating. A minus sign indicates that the issuer's credit standing is deteriorating but has not yet deteriorated far enough to warrant a downgrading of one full notch.

In the case of some municipal bonds, Standard & Poor's issues two other ratings. The first is NCR. It stands for "No contract rating." This means that the issuer has not asked to have its bond rated, although in most cases it has had earlier issues rated.

Historically, unrated bonds have been most apt to enter default. Lack of a rating can, therefore, be a danger sign, although it is not invariably so. Thus the amount of debt being sold may be so small that the issuer believes a rating is not needed, or for some reason the issuer may not want to bear the expense of obtaining a rating.

The other rating is p. It stands for "provisional" and is added to the letter rating that has been awarded. It indicates that Standard & Poor's believes that the bond merits the rating it has been given, but that payment of principal and interest on schedule will be entirely or largely dependent on timely completion of whatever is being built.

The Mechanics of Rating Debt Securities   3

With few exceptions, Standard & Poor's rates all publicly offered corporate bonds and publishes these ratings in its own publications, such as *The Fixed Income Investor* and *The Bond Guide,* in addition to making them available to the general public through various newswire services.* Most of the exceptions involve companies that do not have demonstrable operating records, preferably of 5 years' duration, and companies that do not have audited financial statements.

To rate corporate bonds Standard & Poor's currently employs some 30 analysts. To some extent these analysts specialize in issues sold by companies in particular industries. By and large, however, they are generalists, able to analyze the credit worthiness of one type of company as easily as another.

Ordinarily, two analysts are assigned to study a new issue. They not only study the information with which they have been provided by the issuing corporation—of which more in subsequent chapters—but they also study any historical information in their own files. They also talk with other business sources, including on occasion the issuer's competitors.

---

*Standard & Poor's does not publish its ratings of privately placed debt securities.

More important, they usually talk with the top executives of the issuing company about its past performance and future prospects. Exceptions are sometimes made when a company has brought out a debt issue within, say, the past year or so and no meaningful changes have taken place in its status. Otherwise these meetings are virtually a must.

Sometimes they take place at Standard & Poor's headquarters in New York City. Other times they are held at the issuer's headquarters. If at all possible, the investment advisory organization likes to obtain an impression of a company and its management on their own home ground. Sometimes, however, this is not possible, often because of lack of time.

Once they have completed their research, the analysts meet with three other analysts, at least two of whom must be senior members of the corporate finance department. At these meetings they report their findings and recommend that the issue be given a certain rating. A vote is taken, and majority rule commonly prevails.

This done, the committee reports its recommendations to one of four managers in the corporate finance department. This manager can approve the recommendation or ask the committee to reconsider. In short, he (or she) cannot overrule the committee, but he can compel it to take a second look if he believes it has failed to give proper weight to some important factor pertaining to the bond or the issuing company. Because at least six persons usually consider any single rating, the chances of bias or oversight are virtually negligible.

Despite these efforts, companies that issue bonds do not always agree with Standard & Poor's decisions. If they do not, they may appeal them. Perhaps a fifth of these appeals are upheld and the bonds rated one grade higher. When this happens, it is often because the issuer provides new information that it did not provide when it originally sought a rating. For example, it may supply a more comprehensive breakdown of its sources of earnings.

In addition to allowing appeals, Standard & Poor's reevaluates its ratings of corporate bonds at least once a year. The investment advisory organization studies the most recent annual report put out by each company, plus any other information the company may provide, as well as the annual 10-K and quarterly 10-Q reports it has filed with the Securities & Exchange Commission and any articles about it that have appeared in business and trade journals. The rating agency also carefully considers the financial ratios, such as the ratio of a company's debt

The Mechanics of Rating Debt Securities

to capitalization, which can be so important to a rating. In essence, it looks for important changes in the figures and other factors that caused it to give a bond a certain rating in the first place.

Once this review has been made, a committee may or may not meet, depending on whether a change in rating seems in order. If a change does seem warranted, a meeting is convened. Yet the vote to change the rating must be unanimous or virtually so rather than the expression of a majority. When a change is effected, the new rating will not affect the amount of interest the issuer has to pay on its bonds already outstanding, but it is almost certain to affect the amount of interest that the issuer will have to pay on any bonds it sells in the future.

For rating corporate bonds, Standard & Poor's charges a fee. This fee ordinarily ranges between $2500 and $10,000 and is usually near the midpoint.

The exact size of the fee depends on the amount of time and effort that must be spent to arrive at a rating, plus whether Standard & Poor's performs other services for the issuer. For example, if Standard & Poor's also rates commercial paper sold by the issuer, it reduces its fee for rating the bond offering. That is because it regularly collects information pertaining to the commercial paper, and much of this information is also pertinent to the bond issue.

The amount of the issue also helps govern the size of the fee. Thus the fee declines slightly, on a percentage basis, as the amount of the issue increases.

In the case of utility bonds, the minimum fee is often lower—perhaps $2000 instead of $2500—because many utilities enter the bond market very regularly. For this reason, Standard & Poor's ordinarily finds that it takes less time than usual to rate an individual issue.

It is worth mentioning that more and more companies are seeking a preliminary rating—that is, a rating in advance of filing a prospectus with the SEC. In such cases, Standard & Poor's requires them to provide the same information that they would have to provide if they were seeking a formal rating.

Many companies that take this step have never or only very infrequently issued bonds before. Thus they want to ascertain what kind of rating they are likely to obtain before deciding to go ahead. If the company decides not to proceed, it is still obligated to pay Standard & Poor's for its services on the same basis as other companies. Nonetheless, the fee is apt to be only one-half to two-thirds of what it would ordinarily be, because the investment advisory organization will not have to spend time maintaining surveillance of the bonds.

Now what about commercial paper? The investment advisory organization goes about rating such paper in the same way that it rates bonds. Thus it requests certain information from the potential issuer, then turns this information over to two analysts. Once they have made their study, they meet with three other analysts, recommend that the paper be given a certain rating, and explain their reasoning. The committee then votes on the recommendation, and majority rule prevails.

Juliette L. Gould, who is in charge of Standard & Poor's commercial paper ratings, then reviews the committee's findings and either approves the decision or requests the committee to reconvene and reconsider.

Like bond issuers, commercial paper issuers may also protest—as well as reject—their ratings. Some do protest, and sometimes they are upheld.

On top of all this, Standard & Poor's reviews all its ratings, as in the case of bonds, but it does so quarterly rather than annually. Ratings are changed relatively infrequently. A committee decides if and when to make such a revision. And the decision to do so must be virtually unanimous.

For its services, Standard & Poor's again charges a fee. This fee is payable, regardless or whether the issuer accepts or rejects the investment advisory organization's rating.

For industrial and most other companies, the fee, which in the case of commercial paper is applied annually, ranges between $2500 and $3500, depending on the amount of work required. For utilities the fee is apt to be a little less. As we learned earlier, utilities issue debt with such regularity that it is less laborious than usual for Standard & Poor's to rate any individual security.

The company's municipal bond department operates in much the same fashion as its corporate bond department. Yet there are differences between their operations. Perhaps the chief one is that, unlike the corporate department, the municipal department does not rate virtually all the bonds that fall within its purview. At one point it did so, but since 1968 it has operated on a contract basis and rated only those bonds that states, cities, and various public authorities have asked it to rate.

Even when these public bodies ask, it does not always meet their requests. For example, it does not usually rate revenue bonds whose

The Mechanics of Rating Debt Securities 25

proceeds will be used primarily for recreational purposes. It believes that the revenues generated by such projects are potentially too erratic for it to assess the bonds accurately.

Despite all this, Standard & Poor's does rate the overwhelming majority of municipal bonds, both in terms of number of issues and dollar volume. In both cases, the proportion exceeds 75 percent.

The municipal bond department also differs from the corporate bond department in that it does not usually rate notes that fall within its purview. The exceptions are few and far between.

The reason is simple. It thinks that the real security behind municipal notes lies in their issuers' ability to roll them over—that is, to issue new notes in approximately the same dollar amount when the old ones mature—or else to convert the old notes into long-term bonds. Thus Standard & Poor's believes that if it rated notes, it would, in effect, be rating the issuers' ability to sell new notes, not their ability to make principal and interest payments on those already outstanding. In short, it would be rating the issuers' market worthiness, not their credit worthiness.

What about privately placed municipal bonds? The fact is, very few are privately placed, and of those that are, Standard & Poor's rates only a very small proportion, on request. In so doing, it operates in the same fashion it does in rating public issues.

When it rates public issues, it publishes its decisions and the reasons therefor in *The Fixed Income Investor* and certain of its other publications. It also makes them available to selected financial organizations such as the Dow-Jones Co.

To make municipal ratings Standard & Poor's currently employs 16 analysts. Like the company's corporate analysts, they are by and large generalists, able to rate bonds as well from one state, city, or public authority as another. Commonly, one analyst is assigned to study each issue. If the issue is important or unusual, however, two may be given the job.

Sometimes the analysts recommend a rating solely on the basis of the written information that they have been given. Sometimes they do so only after having talked with state, city, or authority officials at Standard & Poor's headquarters, and sometimes they do so only after visiting the organizations in question. "The last method," observes Robert L. Margolies, an associate manager in the municipal bond department, "gives us a better feel for a community and its physical aspects and also a better idea of management, its capabilities, and its method of running the show."

Once the analysts have completed their research, they meet with a committee of at least five and often seven members and make their recommendations. These committees are perhaps a little less prone than their corporate counterparts to accept the decisions that are occasionally rendered by a bare majority. They like a fuller meeting of minds.

Like corporations, municipalities can appeal the ratings given their bonds. Actually, very few do so. Those that do, however, are given a full hearing, and occasionally Standard & Poor's reverses itself. When it does, the most common reason is that the municipality has disclosed further information about itself that Standard & Poor's had not previously known.

The investment advisory organization endeavors to review all municipal ratings at least annually. In so doing, it checks each municipality's annual audit, the amount of debt it has outstanding, any new legislation that affects it, its economic situation, and its financial operations.

A decision to revise a rating is again made by committee vote. The department likes a strong vote one way or another. The most common reason for a change in rating is a change, whether for better or worse, in a municipality's economic situation or its financial condition.

Standard & Poor's fee for rating municipal bonds is determined by the time and effort required to make a rating. The fees range between $500 and $2500 and typically amount to $750. One reason that this range of fees is markedly lower than that for rating corporate bonds is that in ordinary times general obligation bonds are perhaps the easiest of all bonds to rate. As you may know, they constitute the majority of municipal bonds.

The amount of a municipal issue does not help govern the size of Standard & Poor's fee. The investment advisory organization charges the same for a large issue as a small one, all other things being equal. But if a municipality enters the debt market frequently—say, three or four times a year—Standard & Poor's usually charges less on subsequent issues than it does the first time around. Commonly the fee is at least one-quarter lower than it otherwise would be.

Like corporations, municipalities occasionally seek in advance to ascertain how their bonds are likely to be rated. In such cases they must provide the same information and pay the same fees they would if they had formally requested a rating.

How Industrial Bonds Are Rated   4

Today there are some 4000 corporate bonds outstanding. A study done in 1972 by Salomon Brothers, the well-known investment banking firm, shows that about 26 percent of the total amount outstanding are industrial bonds, which may be defined as corporate bonds issued by manufacturers, retailers, and the like, as opposed to those issued by utilities, banks, other financial firms, or transportation companies.

To obtain a rating a company first contacts Standard & Poor's directly or through an investment banking firm. It is usually better to take the latter course, because a banker knows what Standard & Poor's requires and can, therefore, expedite the rating process.

The information needed includes the following: a preliminary prospectus* or, if this is not available, a letter stipulating the terms of the issue; the most recent 10-K report† that the company has filed with the SEC; annual reports for the past 5 years; quarterly financial statements issued since the last annual report; and in many cases forecasts,

---

*A final prospectus must be provided after the issue has been formally offered to investors. If the terms of the issue differ from those listed in the preliminary prospectus or if the status of the company has changed, Standard & Poor's reserves the right to alter the rating it has given the issue.

†The SEC requires every publicly owned company to file a so-called 10-K report with it yearly. This report must include all the information that the company has included in its most recent annual report, plus certain other data.

for 5 years into the future, of income statements, balance sheets, and source and application of funds statements. These forecasts should be accompanied by a list of assumptions. (For a detailed indication of the best way to submit this information to Standard & Poor's, see the appendix beginning on page 145.)

Once they have this information, Standard & Poor's analysts set to work. We studied the scope of their investigation in the preceding chapter.

What actually do they look at in a proposed industrial bond issue? Five factors stand out. They are the bond's indenture and the issuing company's asset protection, financial resources, future earning power, and management.

An indenture is the basic legal document that spells out the contract between the bond issuer and the bondholders. Standard & Poor's looks at the covenants in the indenture and at the remedies provided for lack of compliance. It is basically interested in the following questions:

- Do the provisions deviate from standard practice? If so, how and why? For example, if a bond from a holding company were involved, the investment advisory organization would expect restrictions to be placed on the right of the company's subsidiaries to issue debt. That's because debt issued by the subsidiaries would have prior claim on the subsidiaries' assets in case of bankruptcy.
- Does the indenture allow the company to issue other bonds that would have an equal or greater claim on its assets than the bond in question? Thus, even if it were not dealing with a holding company, Standard & Poor's might expect certain restrictions to be placed on the company's right to issue further debt. The weaker the credit worthiness of the issuer, the more restrictive the convenants would be expected to be.
- Does the indenture spell out specific standards the company must meet before it can issue other bonds? Standard & Poor's expects an industrial company's adjusted net tangible assets to be at least two and one-half times as large as its pro forma long-term debt if the company's bond issue is to receive an investment-grade rating (triple-B or higher). A company's net tangible assets are equal to the depreciated book value of its plant, property, and equipment, plus the value of all its other assets, plus its working capital, less deferred items, reserves, and all other liabilities. Its pro forma debt includes the amount of the proposed new issue and any debt it already has

outstanding, adjusted for any indebtedness to be repaid out of the proceeds of the proposed new issue.
- Does the indenture include a mortgage on the company's property or a lien on its revenues? These days industrial bonds rarely carry mortgages or liens, but utility bonds often do. For this reason, we look at this point more carefully in Chapter 5.
- Does the indenture require the issuer to set up a sinking fund into which it must put annual contributions toward repayment of principal? Standard & Poor's does not insist on such funds. But it does prefer them and likes the issuer to promise to have retired a very substantial portion of the bond's principal by the time the bond matures.* One reason should be obvious: sinking funds provide for orderly retirement of debt and ensure that a company will not have to pay out a very large sum of money in a single year.
- Are the bonds senior or subordinated? And is there any mortgage or lien debt that ranks ahead of them? If the bonds are subordinated to other indebtedness, then, in the event of bankruptcy or liquidation, the holders of the subordinated bonds will probably receive nothing unless there is enough realizable asset value to at least pay off senior creditors in full. If there is enough such value, the subordinated bondholders will be paid off in full or in part, depending on how much can be realized. In other words, subordinated bonds entail more risk than senior bonds and, other things being equal, ordinarily receive lower ratings than senior issues.
- Is the indenture too restrictive? In other words, does it deprive the company of the flexibility it may need to meet changing economic and competitive conditions? For example, would it prevent the company from making acquisitions or from otherwise expanding if that should seem desirable?

Asset protection is another factor considered by Standard & Poor's and is perhaps the most cut-and-dried of the group. That is because the

---

*In the case of companies in extractive industries like copper, gas, and oil, the investment advisory organization prefers full payouts of principal before maturity by means of sinking fund payments. In addition, it often encourages limitation of the bonds' life (or term) to 20 years or less instead of 30, depending on the remaining useful life of the company's natural resources or its key supplies. This is because the assets of such companies are of value only as they are put to use. In other words, in case of default, the bondholders would recover little of immediate worth.

degree to which a company's debt is covered by the value of its assets can in large measure be determined by four ratios.

The first ratio relates the company's pro forma long-term debt to its net property, plant, and equipment. For a bond to qualify for a triple- or double-A rating, the debt should be less than 50 percent of net property, plant, and equipment; for a single-A rating, less than 75 percent; and for a triple-B rating, not much more than 100 percent.

The second ratio relates working capital to pro forma long-term debt. For a bond to qualify for a triple- or double-A rating, working capital should equal or exceed the debt; for a single-A rating, if should be equal to 65 or 75 percent of the debt; and for a triple-B rating, if should be equal to 45 to 50 percent of the debt.

The third ratio relates pro forma long-term debt to equity or, as the ratio is commonly referred to, debt to capitalization. In this case for a bond to qualify for a triple-A rating, debt should be no more than 25 percent of capitalization; for a double-A rating, no more than 30 percent; for a single-A rating, no more than 35 percent; and for a triple-B rating, no more than 45 percent.

The final ratio relates net tangible assets to pro forma long-term debt. When corporate net assets cover the debt by four or five to one, a bond is a candidate for a triple-A rating; when by three and one-half to four to one, for a double-A rating; when by three to three and one-half to one, for a single-A rating; and when by two and one-half to three to one, for a triple-B rating. But remember these three qualifications:

First, these ratios are not applied inflexibly. Rather they are ratios that typical companies must meet to be candidates for a given rating. In other words, many exceptions apply, particularly in certain industries.

For example, the ratios would be much less important to a publisher than to a manufacturer, because the former does not have much plant and equipment. Its assets consist of titles, copyrights, and the like. Therefore, in its case, the significant questions become: How much is the company earning on its assets, and how well are these earnings protected?

Second, merely because a company has asset-protection ratios sufficient to qualify its bonds for a rating of, say, double-A does not guarantee that the bonds will receive this rating. Strong ratios may be offset by weaknesses in other areas, and vice versa.

Finally, although they are important, these ratios are not the only facet of asset protection that Standard & Poor's looks at. It also asks:

How Industrial Bonds Are Rated

- What is the makeup of the company's working capital? Working capital, of course, consists of current assets minus current liabilities, the latter being those liabilities payable within 1 year. The greater the proportion of cash assets or assets easily convertible into cash (such as readily marketable securities or factorable receivables) as opposed to less liquid assets (such as inventories and prepaid expenses), the healthier the company is deemed to be. Of course, there can be instances in which a company's marketable securities cannot be sold quickly, except at substantial discounts, in which case their value will not be as great as it seems. There can also be instances in which inventories can be readily convertible into cash.
- What is the book value of the company's assets, and can this value be justified? If book value is far in excess of known or estimated market value, not only the company's assets but also its accounting system comes into question. Perhaps an inadequate amount of depreciation is being taken, thus boosting current earnings at the expense of building up an adequate depreciation reserve for future replacement of fixed assets.
- What is the quality of the company's inventories? If they are obsolete or even somewhat dated, their real value may be less than is listed.
- What is the character of the property account, which consists of plant, equipment, land, and other fixed assets? Standard & Poor's asks: How new are the facilities? How competitive? How many improvements have been made in them in the last 5 years? And how much is the company spending to keep its plant in shape? If the company is not spending an amount at least equal to what it is taking in depreciation and if it has not made any improvements in recent years, a big question usually arises in the minds of the analysts. Of course, there can be cases in which a fully mature company in an industry that requires less capital investment than most does not need to make substantial capital outlays.

All these questions are important. In other words, the four asset-protection ratios we looked at earlier can be considered only after these questions have been answered.

Before turning our attention from asset protection to financial resources, let us pause to consider one other matter affecting a company's capital structure. It involves leasing and other methods of so-called off-balance sheet financing. In recent years leasing has become big business. Some estimates put the capitalized value of all outstanding leases in this country at $80 billion.

Leasing involves payments that are part interest and part principal. The catch is, most companies do not capitalize these obligations on their balance sheets, although many do include them in footnotes to the sheets. The result is that such companies have balance sheets that look better than they actually are. In other words, their debt to equity ratios, to cite one example, are lower than they would be if the leases were capitalized.

What is Standard & Poor's attitude toward these companies? The answer is simple: If the lease payments are minor, it does not penalize the companies for balance-sheet purposes. But if the payments are substantial, it capitalizes them on the balance sheet at 10 times gross rentals in the case of real estate and seven times in the case of personal property.

In a sense, therefore, it makes little difference whether a company seeking a rating capitalizes its lease obligations. If they have any meaningful effect on its balance sheet, this effect will be reflected in the overall rating assigned to the company's securities.

The third factor that Standard & Poor's considers in trying to arrive at a rating is a company's financial resources, in particular its cash and other working capital. These resources provide a good indication of how capable a company is of surviving a recession without defaulting and of financing improvements without further borrowing. Such resources are particularly important in cyclical industries like the steel industry.

In studying a company's working capital, Standard & Poor's weighs several ratios. These include working capital to pro forma long-term debt, working capital to net plant, and others. Essentially, the investment advisory organization is interested in the trend of the company's ratios over a period of years and in how the ratios stack up against those of comparable firms.

Standard & Poor's also examines the quality of the company's current assets: the rate at which it turns over inventory, the rate at which it collects accounts receivable, and the accounting methods it uses to value these two items. There are no industry-wide standards on these matters. An inventory-turnover ratio that might be rapid in one industry could be slow in another. As a result, Standard & Poor's compares the ratios of one company with those of other companies in the same industry.

In addition, the investment advisory organization studies a

company's dividend policies. Because policies vary from one industry to another, there is no nationwide guideline as to what constitutes reasonable payouts. Once again, Standard & Poor's compares a company's policies with those of its competitors. As you can guess, it is wary of a company whose dividends seem too generous, especially if its capital expenditures and its debt are increasing. Overly generous dividends may indicate that the company is not protecting itself sufficiently against possible future economic uncertainty.

Is the company relying too heavily—or likely to have to rely too heavily in the near future—on external financing because it is not building up its retained earnings adequately? Standard & Poor's is especially wary of companies that make excessive use of short-term debt and that carry a permanent wedge of such debt instead of prudently funding the long-term portion as appropriate. In such cases the investment advisory organization works up pro forma ratios by transferring all or part of the short-term indebtedness to the long-term sector or by computing the company's ratios on a total debt basis.

The company's use of other external financial resources is also important. Thus Standard & Poor's is certain to ask: How big are the company's bank loans? How long have they been outstanding? Has the company been too dependent on banks? Will it be able to come back to the long-term debt market in the reasonably near future, if necessary? Or will it be so top-heavy with debt that investors would shy away from its bonds or demand huge rates of interest? Thus, as Leo O'Neill, vice president of Standard & Poor's corporate bond department, puts it: "We are interested not just in the size of a company's financial resources but also in their character."

A company's estimated future earnings are of great importance to its bond's rating. "Today," emphasizes O'Neill, "both the level and quality of a company's profits are crucial. Obviously, it is better to invest in a company that earns enough to pay off principal and interest than to have first claim on its assets in case of default."

To ascertain a company's future earning power, Standard & Poor's first considers the industry it is in. Is it a growth industry, or is it a stable, mature one? Are the industry's long-term sales and earnings trends moving upward or downward or holding steady? Is demand for its products constant or cyclical?

Standard & Poor's also studies the company's position in the industry. Is the company a leader and, therefore, likely to have a strong impact on industry policies, practices, and prices? If it is not a leader, has it increased its share of the market in recent years? And again, if not, has it at least increased its sales and earnings? Has it also reduced some of its cost ratios, such as the amount of property or labor needed to produce a dollar of sales?

Another area that the investment advisory organization looks into is the company's depreciation practices. There are no fixed guidelines on this matter, partly because the nature of properties and other assets vary sharply from industry to industry, partly because depreciation practices do so, too. Once again, Standard & Poor's compares the practices of the company in question with those of its competitors. Naturally, it is skeptical of companies that set aside too little toward depreciation and, therefore, inflate their earnings.

Not surprisingly, Standard & Poor's also weighs a company's tax practices. It is especially interested in whether investment tax credits are taken in the year in which they are realized or over the life of the asset. The method employed will have a direct influence on present and future earnings. Says Roy Weinberger, one of the managers in Standard & Poor's corporate bond department: "Many companies take the tax credit immediately. But, as in so many other matters, we prefer a conservative, long-range approach whereby the credit is spread over the life of the asset."

The adequacy of a company's financial controls also helps govern its earnings potential. Standard & Poor's wants to be sure that there is some central authority that oversees the company's divisions or departments and evaluates or approves their plans, in addition to reviewing the results thereof.

Does the company also conduct stringent internal audits? Believe it or not, many firms do not do so. As a result, they sometimes suffer from unhappy surprises. Standard & Poor's is almost certain to look askance at a company that does not employ this procedure.

What is the company's cash flow in relation to its long-term debt and any short-term debt that is not being regularly retired? The company's cash flow consists of its net income, plus whatever it is setting aside for depreciation. Ordinarily, Standard & Poor's likes a reasonable balance between income and depreciation.

To have a bond qualify for a triple-A rating, an industrial company would commonly have to have cash flow equal to at least 75 percent of its long-term debt; for a double-A rating, cash flow equal to at least 45

How Industrial Bonds Are Rated

percent of the debt; for a single-A rating, cash flow equal to at least 35 percent; and for a triple-B rating, cash flow equal to at least 25 percent.

Finally, in studying future earning power, Standard & Poor's looks at the company's fixed-charge coverage—that is, the number of times its earnings exceed the interest it must pay. In fact, it looks at the current, past, and probable future rate of coverage.

In so doing, it studies at least three ratios. One is interest coverage before taxes. Another is interest coverage after taxes. Possibly the most important is interest and rental coverage after taxes.

For a company's bonds to be a candidate for a triple-A rating, earnings should be seven or eight times as large as interest and rental charges after taxes; for a double-A rating, four or five times as large; for a single-A rating, more than three times; and for a triple-B rating, more than two times.

It must be stressed that although cash flow to debt and fixed-charge coverage ratios are very important, they are not all-important. Thus a company may have fixed-charge coverage that qualifies its bond issue for, say, a single-A rating. Despite this, the bond may actually receive a higher or lower rating, depending on how it stands in relation to all the other factors Standard & Poor's considers.

Much of the information gathered up to this point deals with a company's past. But the past is important only as it sheds light on the future. To obtain more such light, Standard & Poor's almost always wants to talk with management. Says Leo O'Neill: "We are concerned with the philosophy, experience, maturity, capability, and depth of management. For example, if management frequently has to go outside its own ranks for new executives, we would be concerned that it might lack sufficient depth in its senior executive ranks. And we would be alert to the possibility that this may indicate a significant change in the company's direction."

Naturally, the investment advisory organization probes a considerable number of other matters, including:

- What are management's policies and goals? How does it plan to implement and achieve them? If it has been in office for some years, how successful has it been in implementing and accomplishing these things in the past?
- What funds will management have to raise externally to achieve its goals? Are its estimates realistic?

- In this connection, what are management's cash-flow projections for the next 5 years? Although a company cannot accurately project such figures much more than a year or so ahead, Standard & Poor's likes to see longer projections, because they help to illustrate the company's objectives.
- What are management's plans for the immediate future? "Top executives sometimes make glowing predictions of what their company will be like 4 or 5 years down the road," says Leo O'Neill. "But these are sometimes extrapolated from near-term objectives."
- Has management provided for unforeseen events? In other words, does it have a reserve fund and other plans to deal with unexpected contingencies?
- What is the company's philosophy about acquisitions? Although Standard & Poor's has no bias against acquisitions, it is aware that many companies got into trouble a few years ago by seeming to make acquisitions for acquisition's sake and by plunging into fields they knew nothing about.
- What are its new product plans? To assess the efficacy of these plans, Standard & Poor's likes to check the company's new product record in the past.
- What is the company spending on research and development? The investment advisory organization is usually concerned if the company is not spending approximately as much, relative to its sales, as the leaders in its industry.
- What is the company's advertising program? Standard & Poor's analysts do not profess to be advertising experts. But they can discern between phenomenally successful and run-of-the-mill campaigns as well as anyone else.

This list of questions is not necessarily all-inclusive, but it contains many of the major queries the analysts tend to pose. Obviously, their assessment of the answers they are given must be judgemental—if you like, subjective. Against this, they are in a position to compare the answers of many different managements to the same questions. This helps put their judgement on a more objective basis than otherwise might be the case.

Now let us put all this information to practical application and see how Standard & Poor's rated the bonds of two well-known companies at a fairly recent point in time.

How Industrial Bonds Are Rated

In 1970 Federated Department Stores issued $50 million of 25-year sinking fund debentures. As Standard & Poor's saw it, the company was a leader in its industry, and the industry was fairly consistent. In addition, the company was well dispersed geographically, and its earnings had been consistently good. Furthermore, its working capital totaled $3.26 for every $1 of proposed debt. Its cash flow was equal to 95 percent of this debt, and its net tangible assets amounted to $6.36 for every $1 of debt. As you can surmise, its bond issue was given a triple-A rating.

United States Steel is the protagonist of a story with a less happy ending. Its bonds once carried a double-A rating. But when Standard & Poor's reviewed this rating in 1970, it noted that the company's long-term debt had increased almost threefold, that its net tangible assets to debt ratio had dipped below the preferred minimum, and that its earnings had been very erratic.

Despite this, Standard & Poor's decided to maintain the rating. This was partly because the steel manufacturer had been going through a period of planned refurbishment, partly because its raw materials were grossly undervalued. Actually, the company had enough supplies on hand to function for 40 years.

But then earnings continued to decline, further weakening the company's fixed-charge coverage. And in 1971, Standard & Poor's felt compelled to cut the rating on U.S. Steel bonds to single-A, where it still stands as of this writing.

The indenture, asset protection, financial resources, future earning power, and management; these then are the five major areas that Standard & Poor's looks at in rating an industrial bond. As you can see, the job is complex and requires consideration of many different facets of corporate operations. In addition, it demands discernment on both objective and subjective levels.

How Other Corporate Financing Vehicles Are Rated 5

Before discussing how utility bonds are rated, let us pause to consider very briefly six other methods of corporate financing and how these vehicles are rated. These issues include intermediate-term bonds, corporate notes, convertible bonds, preferred stock, private placements, and lease-related financing. Although none of these issues is as common as conventional long-term bonds are, they are all common enough and well known both to the professional investment community and, by and large, to individual investors as well. We can discuss these issues briefly because the job of rating them is essentially no different than that of rating long-term bonds.

Intermediate-term Bonds

Historically, bonds have been issued for periods ranging from 5 years to perpetuity. Yet the majority are issued for from 20 to 30 years and, as such, are known as long-term bonds.

By contrast, intermediate-term—or medium-term—bonds are usually issued for from 5 to 10 years. Indeed, their maturity is the only important difference between them and long-term bonds, and it might not be worth mentioning them at all if they had not become very popular in the last half-dozen years.

The strength of the trend has been pronounced. Thus in 1971 intermediate-term corporate financing represented only 14 percent of the total of straight bond financing. In 1972 this figure jumped to 22 percent. Then, after dipping sharply in 1973, it shot up to 31 percent in 1974 and, as this is written, is still climbing.

Interestingly, the bonds are proving popular both with companies with high credit ratings and those with lower ones. In fact, some well-known companies, such as du Pont and Xerox, have brought out long-term and intermediate-term issues simultaneously. This saves on interest and gives the issues broad appeal.

There are several other reasons for the trend toward intermediate-term issues. Some apply to the corporations that issue them, some to the organizations and individuals who invest in them.

The impetus for the spread of this kind of issue comes from tight money. The absence of easy credit in the early 1970s pushed up interest rates sharply, and many companies simply did not want to commit themselves to paying such high rates for 20 or more years.

What's more, intermediate-term issues usually carry significantly lower rates of interest than long-term issues, even in periods of tight money. The reasons are simple. Investors in such issues tie up their money for a considerably shorter period of time than would otherwise be the case and are, therefore, willing to accept a lower rate of interest in exchange for being able to reinvest their funds earlier at what may be a higher rate of interest. Also, the issuers of such debt have use of the money for substantially less time than they ordinarily would and may have to refinance the debt later on at a higher rate of interest. Thus they are not willing to pay as high a rate as they would be if they could lock in a set rate for 20 or 30 years.

Despite their difference in maturity, intermediate-term issues are rated in the same fashion as long-term issues. The issuers must supply the same kind and amount of information to Standard & Poor's. And the latter organization considers the same factors—indenture, asset protection, financial resources, future earning power, and management—as it would if it were assaying 20- or 30-year bonds.

The only other important questions it asks are: Where will the issuing company get the money to pay off the bond issue? Is there an adequate sinking fund? After all, 8 or 10 years pass by much more quickly than 20 or 30. Yet presuming these questions are answered satisfactorily,

How Other Corporate Financing Vehicles Are Rated

intermediate-term bonds do not ordinarily suffer a lower rating or enjoy a higher one than would long-term bonds issued by the same company at the same point in time.

Corporate Notes

Corporate notes are much like intermediate-term bonds and, in fact, have historically been more common. They, too, basically differ from long-term bonds only in that they are issued for shorter periods of time.

Many investors think of corporate notes as having a maturity of no more than seven years. That is probably because United States Treasury notes have usually been issued for that or shorter terms. Actually, corporate notes are often issued for up to 10 years, and in 1974 General Foods went so far as to issue $100 million of 14-year notes.

Notes are popular for the same reasons that intermediate-term bonds are. The issuer does not have to commit itself to pay a high rate of interest for an extended period of time. Nor does the investor have to tie up his money for two or three decades.

Sometimes an additional factor is at work. A company's intermediate-term outlook may seem sanguine, but its long-term outlook may be less certain. In other words, potential investors may be more likely to buy 10-year notes than 20-year bonds.

In any case, once again, the issuer must supply the same information as it would in the case of a long-term issue. And Standard & Poor's will ask the same questions, wondering in addition only how all the money that will be borrowed can be paid off in a relatively short period of time.

And once again, corporate notes are likely to receive the same rating as would long-term bonds issued by the same company at the same point in time. Exceptions are made only in cases where the notes are made subordinate to bonds already outstanding or about to be issued. In such cases the notes are almost invariably rated one notch lower than the bonds.

Convertible Bonds

As you know, these bonds are convertible into common or occasionally preferred stock. For this reason, they differ from conventional long-term bonds much more markedly than intermediate-term bonds and corporate notes do. They also operate in the secondary market much differently than conventional bonds do. Their prices are apt to go up and down more frequently, rapidly and sharply.

Nevertheless, convertible bonds are rated in almost exactly the same fashion that conventional bonds are. The reason is simple. Standard & Poor's gives no weight whatsoever to the fact that these bonds can be converted into stock. It is interested only in the two questions it is always interested in: Can the issuer pay back what it borrows when it is supposed to do so? Can it pay interest on schedule?

When convertible bonds are not made subordinate to any straight bonds the issuer may have outstanding, they are likely to receive the same ratings as the straight bonds. Yet most convertibles are made subordinate to other bonds and, therefore, are usually rated one notch lower. When a company already has a great deal of either senior or subordinated debt outstanding, they may be rated two notches lower.

Preferred Stock

This stock, of course, is equity rather than debt. Nonetheless, Standard & Poor's rates it in much the same fashion as bonds and uses the same symbols, with virtually the same meanings, to do so. In fact, there are really only two major differences between rating preferred stocks and rating bonds.

First, the stock affects the statistical ratios that Standard & Poor's employs to help assess the credit worthiness of the issuer. In other words, the ratios are adjusted to take account of the stock.

For example, as we saw in the previous chapter, a bond issue will ordinarily be a candidate for a triple-A rating if its earnings exceed its interest and rental payments seven or eight times over. But for preferred stock to be eligible for such a rating, earnings must exceed bond interest, preferred stock dividends, and rental payments only five or six times over.

Second, Standard & Poor's wants to ascertain the status of the stock in the issuer's capital structure. If the issuer has only a small amount of debt outstanding, it is a good sign.

In any case in most instances the stock receives the same rating as the issuer's bonds or, more commonly, a rating one notch lower. The more debt the issuer has outstanding, the more likely it is that the stock will be rated lower.

It is important to understand that, in rating preferred stock, Stan-

How Other Corporate Financing Vehicles Are Rated

dard & Poor's always compares it with like stock from similar companies. Thus the preferred stock is not assessed within a one-company vacuum but is judged within the total universe of preferred stocks.

Private Placements

These securities simply represent debt or equity that is sold to no more than 50 to 100 private investors instead of being brought to public market where they would be made available to all investors. Almost invariably, such securities are sold to large institutional investors like life insurance companies and pension funds.

The issuers of these securities usually have to pay more interest than they would if they sold the securities publicly. How much more depends on the supply of capital available in the public and private markets at any given time and related factors. As of now, most issuers of private placements have to pay from one-quarter to one-half percent more in interest than they would in the public market.

Despite this, private placements are a popular method of raising capital. There are several reasons why.

For one thing, a private placement cuts red tape and saves time. Among other reasons, the issuer does not have to register the securities with the SEC. Also, a private placement avoids public disclosure of corporate information. In other words, the issuer may be willing to tell private institutional investors about certain aspects of its affairs, but it may not want to divulge these same matters to a wider audience.

For a third thing, a private placement provides flexibility. Both buyer and seller can tailor the terms of the issue to their individual needs.

Twenty-five years ago the public and private placement markets for corporate bonds were roughly equal in size, but a gap has slowly arisen between them. Today, the public market is more than twice as large as the private market, although naturally the exact ratio in new issues may vary sharply from year to year.

Standard & Poor's probably rates less than 25 percent of the total dollar volume of those privately placed securities issued each year. The reason is, most institutional investors are experienced buyers of both public and privately placed bond issues, and they have people on their own staffs well equipped to evaluate such issues from the standpoint of relative safety of principal and interest.

When the investment advisory organization does rate such issues, it does so only on request. Often such requests come from institutional investors that do not have analysts of their own.

In any case Standard & Poor's looks at the same factors and asks the same questions about private placements as it does about public issues. Because it is under no obligation to maintain continuing surveillance of private issues, it usually does not charge as much as it does for rating public issues. Ordinarily its fees range from $600 to $7500 and average about two-thirds as much as they do for public issues.

Lease-related Financing

Leasing is increasingly popular with business because most companies can keep this kind of debt off their balance sheets. This method of financing may involve real property (real estate) or personal property (buildings, equipment, and the like). It may consist of straight sale and leasebacks, industrial revenue bonds, pollution-control bonds, or similar channels, and it may be either private or public.

Leases can be and frequently are sold or traded, just as other kinds of debt are. Standard & Poor's rates perhaps 200 of them a year, only on request, and does so both for the benefit of whoever holds the debt portion of a lease and the lessee.

What does the investment advisory organization look at in rating leases?

First, it wants to know how much equity has been put up—that is, how much money is being invested in whatever is being leased versus how much of the cost is being borrowed. The equity may be put up by the lessor, the lessee, or some third party. Whoever does the job, Standard & Poor's usually expects 20 to 25 percent of the total cost to be in the form of equity and an even higher amount in the case of lessees whose senior debt ratings are in any danger of being downgraded.

Second, it looks at all the factors it investigates in rating a bond—save the indenture. Thus it checks the company's asset protection, financial resources, future earning power, and management. It applies the same standards that it does in the case of bonds.

Third, it looks at the terms of the lease, which are the equivalent of the indenture on a bond. The lease rental payments may constitute the only source of repayment. Or the lease may be secured by both lease

How Other Corporate Financing Vehicles Are Rated

rental payments and a mortgage or security interest in the property. Or it may be secured by both the lease rental payments and an unconditional guarantee from a parent firm that these payments will be made.

The nature of the lease helps determine whether it will be accorded the same status as the lessee's senior or subordinated debt, if any. Obviously, the stronger the terms, the more likely it is that the lease will be rated the same as the company's senior debt.

In checking the terms of the lease, Standard & Poor's also wants to make sure that the lease payments provide for full payment of the debt over the life of the lease. In other words, the investment advisory organization would look askance at a company if its lease extended for, say, 10 years, yet only a portion of this debt would be paid off by the end of this period.

One other point is of importance. If the lease involves real property, then a "one-to-three years' rentals" rule may apply in case of bankruptcy. In other words a court may award the lessor only this much in lease or rental payments if the lessee goes bankrupt. This rule does not usually apply, however, in the case of property leases.

Finally, Standard & Poor's looks at the rating that it has given any senior debt the lessee may have. If everything else is in order and if the protection afforded the holder of the lease is similar to that afforded the holder of senior debt, the rating given the lease is not likely to be different from that given the senior debt.

Before ending this chapter, I want to emphasize one other point. Although I have discussed these six kinds of securities as they relate to industrial issuers, virtually everything I have said applies to other kinds of issuers. For example, Standard & Poor's rates a utility company's notes in the same fashion as it rates the utility's bonds. And it rates a transportation company's convertible bonds in the same fashion as it rates its conventional bonds.

How Utility Bonds Are Rated   6

There are some 275 investor-owned utilities of all kinds in this country, and most of them have both long-term and short-term debt outstanding. Indeed, the study done in 1972 by Salomon Brothers shows that utility issues account for some 59 per cent of the total value of corporate bond issues.

Historically, these bonds have had the best record of all corporate issues and have, therefore, usually received favorable ratings. Thus in late 1972 some 90 percent of all utility issues carried a rating of single-A or better. By contrast, only 83 percent of all corporate issues were rated this highly.

But times are changing. Just in the last few years many utilities have come under serious financial pressure. Their earnings have not kept pace with their need for debt financing. As a result, the degree of protection behind their assets has eroded, too.

The causes of this pressure have been multiple. Inflation is the primary one. A decline in consumer demand is another. The necessity of expending more funds to combat pollution is a third. And the length of time that many public service commissions take to approve increases in utility rates is a fourth. This list could well be extended.

Whatever the causes of a given utility's financial woes, Standard & Poor's has had to lower its ratings on a sizable number of utility issues. Indeed, in 1974 alone the investment advisory organization reduced its ratings on the first-mortgage bonds of five of the seven utilities that serve the state of Ohio.

All is not lost to the utilities by any means. Some utility issues carry higher ratings than they once did, but the industry in general, particularly the electric utility industry, continues to face long-term stress. Only time will tell how it will fare.

In rating utility issues, Standard & Poor's looks at the same five factors it considers in rating industrial issues: indenture, asset protection, financial resources, future earning power, and management. It also asks most of the same questions it asks of industrial companies. Nevertheless, utility companies have special facets and problems. We must look at these five factors carefully.

In studying utility indentures, Standard & Poor's poses many of the questions you would expect: Does the indenture allow the utility to issue debt senior to the debt in question? Does it establish specific standards the utility must meet before it can issue additional debt? Does it require establishment of a sinking, property, or maintenance fund? And so forth. Yet, in general, the analysts ordinarily spend less time on utility indentures than they do on those pertaining to other kinds of issues, because the former tend to be very cut-and-dried.

Nevertheless, there is at least one important difference between utility bond and industrial bond indentures. Most industrial bonds issued these days are debentures, backed only by the general reputation and credit worthiness of their issuers. By contrast, most utility bonds are mortgage bonds, backed by general liens on the assets or revenues of the issuers.

Naturally, Standard & Poor's wants to know just how adequately these assets are protected. In particular, it is interested in the limitations on the amount of additional debt that a utility can issue. Usually an indenture forbids a utility from issuing additional debt if its pretax earnings would then cover the fixed charges on its debt by less than a two-to-one margin. In considering a utility's asset protection, Standard & Poor's again asks some of the same questions it asks of industrial companies. The main question it is concerned with is how new, competitive, and shipshape the utility's plant and equipment are.

The analysts then turn to the statistical ratios that do so much to indicate how well assets are protected. In the case of industrial bonds, as you know, the analysts study four ratios. But in the case of utility bonds, they study only three.

How Utility Bonds Are Rated

They do not study a utility's working capital to debt ratio because ordinarily a utility cannot pay off long-term debt out of working capital. This is because a new plant provides no return on investment until it is actually put into operation. So, to pay off old debt utilities must commonly issue new.

They study a utility's debt to assets ratio essentially to see what limits are placed on the utility's right to issue additional debt. Often utilities are barred from issuing debt in excess of 60 percent of the value of their net tangible assets.

That leaves two ratios. In both cases, Standard & Poor's applies different criteria than it applies to industrial issues. This is because utilities are regulated monopolies and as such can carry more leverage—that is, more debt in relation to equity—than industrial companies, which are usually highly subject to competitive forces.

The first ratio relates debt to total capitalization. For a utility to be a candidate for a triple-A rating, its pro forma long-term debt should not amount to more than 50 percent of its capitalization; for a double-A rating, to more than 55 percent; for a single-A rating to more than 58 percent; and for a triple-B rating, to more than 60 percent.*

The second ratio relates current proposed debt to net plant assets. For a bond to be eligible for a triple-A rating, debt should amount to less than 50 percent of the value of net plant assets; for a double-A rating, to 55 percent or less; for a single-A rating to 60 percent or less; and for a triple-B rating, to 65 percent or less.

As usual, these criteria are not applied rigidly. A utility can compensate in other areas for weaknesses in this one, and vice versa.

Standard & Poor's is quite aware of the amount of leasing that many utilities are doing. Indeed, Thomas G. Fendrich, an associate manager in the company's corporate finance department, terms the trend toward leasing discouraging. "Some utilities," he emphasizes, "have overtaxed their borrowing capacity and tried to take the path of least resistance."

For just this reason, the investment advisory organization employs

---

*We learned in the last chapter that Standard & Poor's is apt to be concerned if an industrial company carries a substantial amount of short-term debt past seasonal needs and gives little intention of retiring it or funding it on a long-term basis. The same is true in the case of utilities. When they do so, the investment advisory organization is almost certain to relate total debt—that is, both pro forma long-term debt and short-term debt—to total capitalization. In so doing, the rating agency is likely to study the average amount of such debt outstanding over the preceding year rather than the amount outstanding at any given point in time.

the same procedure it does in the case of leases held by industrial companies. If the rentals are minor in amount, it disregards them. But if they are more than minor, it capitalizes them.

Financial resources, both internal and external, are as important to a utility as to any other company. Thus Standard & Poor's looks first at the quality of the utility's assets and the relative size of its cash flows. In both cases it is especially interested in how the utility stacks up against comparable companies.

The utility's relations with banks are also weighed. In addition, Standard & Poor's investigates a utility's financial flexibility. How much financing will the utility require over the next 5 years? Is its program manageable? How much flexibility is built into it? If the answers to these questions are unsatisfactory or even uncertain, they will have a negative impact on the rating. That's because a utility almost always spends much more than it takes in and because it must usually borrow from the capital markets quite frequently.

This factor becomes particularly important when you remember that the whole capital structure of many utilities has changed markedly just within the past half-dozen or so years. In the early 1960s many utilities generated 50 percent or more of their financial resources internally. But inflation and the long lead times required to construct nuclear plants, among other things, has brought this figure down to 30 or even 20 percent in a number of cases.

It is when we turn to future earning power that we find major differences arising between the way Standard & Poor's weighs a utility bond and the way it weighs an industrial bond. It is not that the investment advisory organization does not look for similarly strong protection in both cases. Rather, it is that many factors affecting this protection are different.

Once again, the analysts first check the type of company they are dealing with—that is, whether it is an electric, gas, telephone, or other kind of utility. They also analyze the demand for its services and are apt to be concerned if growth in demand is too rapid because, in this era of inflation, the company may find it difficult to achieve its allowed rate of return.

As Roy Weinberger, a manager in the corporate finance department, puts it: "In the absence of adequate and timely rate relief, above-average sales growth can very quickly force a utility into a financial straitjacket. Increasingly, sales projections must be considered in conjunction with the regulatory climate in which a utility operates and with its operating conditions. The latter must be conducive to satisfactory progress in earnings and to maintenance of financial flexibility."

Naturally, the analysts also probe the quality of the utility's service, as reflected in such things as the number of customer complaints, and the efficiency of its operations, as reflected in rate comparisons, number of employees per customer and related matters. In addition, they study its public image, as well as the adequacy of its facilities, its maintenance standards, and its accounting practices. In the last instance, they want to be sure that the utility is taking enough in depreciation because of the effect of depreciation on earnings. They also prefer conservative accounting practices, as reflected by the so-called normalization rather than the flow-through method. In essence, normalization involves taking tax credits over the life of an asset rather than all in one year.

The territory in which the utility operates also comes under scrutiny. Points out Roy Weinberger: "The absence or existence of center-city urban problems can have a definite impact on earnings. Generally, utilities with such problems find it more difficult to obtain satisfactory rate relief, incur higher costs, and are uncertain about the long-term viability of their service areas. On the other hand, some such utilities serve a growing and dependent suburban market."

A utility's geographical location will also affect the amount of fuel or other energy it needs, and its customer density per square mile will govern the demands on its personnel and facilities. The political atmosphere in the territory—in particular, whether the public favors utility growth or not—can also affect earnings, as can the economic mix of the business. Utilities that have a good balance among residential, commercial and industrial customers are in a better position to weather recessions.

The analysts also study the utility's construction program and, to this end, have reams of files bearing on its past programs as well as those of other utilities to use as benchmarks. How detailed is the planning for the program? How well has inflation been taken into consideration? Is the proposed new plant or other structure likely to run afoul of conservationists and other ecology-minded groups? Will the company still be a buyer of power after the construction is completed? Standard & Poor's is likely to ask these and many other questions.

In considering a utility's future earning power, the analysts also weigh the regulatory climate in which the utility operates. "Indeed," says Roy Weinberger, "regulation is the key to the earnings and, in many ways, the ratings achieved by all utilities. An unreasonable regulatory commission can bring a utility to its knees in only three or four years."

As a result, the analysts ask: How well does the utility communicate with its regulators? How sophisticated are the regulators? How understanding? What is the political and consumer climate in which they must operate? What guidelines do they use for considering rate increases? How rapidly do they reach decisions on such increases? Many utilities complain that they lose millions of dollars annually because public service commissions take months or even years to approve rate increases.

Says Thomas Fendrich: "Although we do not discuss particular regulatory commissions in public, privately we place them into one of several categories—reasonable, unsatisfactory, and poor."

This done, the analysts look at the utility's fixed-charge coverage ratio. And as in the case of industrial bonds, they view this ratio in several different ways.

In this connection it is important to understand a particular term in use in the utility industry—AFDC (allowance for funds used during construction). It simply refers to a noncash credit that utilities are allowed to add to their incomes to reflect imputed earnings on construction in progress. Importantly, the utilities may require large rate increases to replace such noncash earnings with cash earnings when the plant under construction is actually placed in service.

Standard & Poor's studies the fixed-charge coverage ratio in four ways—before and after taxes and, in both cases, with and without the allowance included. Perhaps the most important is the ratio that reflects fixed-charge coverage before taxes and with the allowance included in income.

In this case for a bond to be eligible for a triple-A rating, its issuer should earn enough to cover total fixed charges at least four times; for it to be eligible for a double-A rating, earnings should exceed fixed charges at least three and one-half times; for a single-A rating, between three and two and three-quarter times; and for a triple-B rating, between two and one-quarter and two times. As usual, these guidelines are not applied so rigidly as to preclude consideration of the numerous other factors that could push the bond's rating up or down.

Finally, of course, the analysts look at management. If anything, they may look at it even more closely than they look at the managements of

How Utility Bonds Are Rated 53

industrial companies. The reason: a number of utilities have come under fire in recent years for alleged inefficiency.

Whatever the truth of this charge, Standard & Poor's asks, basically, the same questions it asks of other managements, questions that are detailed in Chapter 4: What is management's philosophy? What is it trying to do? How will it achieve its goals? What will the implementation cost? And so forth.

Now let us compare what we have learned against two recent ratings. In both cases the regulatory atmosphere in which the issuing companies operate played a major role in determining how their bonds were rated.

In May 1975 Florida Power & Light issued $100 million of first-mortgage bonds. At the time it was expected that the utility will have to issue substantial additional amounts of securities in both 1976 and 1977.

As a result of the May 1975 issue, the utility's long-term debt increased to more than 57 percent of its total capitalization, which is on the high side. Furthermore, its fixed-charge coverage had been declining sharply over a period of several years.

Nevertheless, the utility had won several appeals for permanent increases in its rates, and Standard & Poor's believed these increases would reverse the decline in fixed-charge coverage. Accordingly, it rated the issue A, the same rating it had granted the company's other recent long-term debt issues.

Appalachian Power, which operates in Virginia and West Virginia, was not so fortunate. In April 1975 it brought forth $40 million of first-mortgage bonds.

With this issue, the company's long-term debt represented 60 percent of its capitalization. Additionally, its fixed-charge coverage had dropped significantly in 1974. "And," noted Standard & Poor's, "the company's ability to finance necessary, continuing construction programs has been restricted as a result of delays in obtaining rate increases, an inadequacy in the rate increases that have been granted, expenditures for pollution-control facilities, and increased capital and operating costs." Accordingly, the investment advisory organization rated Appalachian's new bond issue only triple-B. In addition, it lowered its ratings on all the rest of the company's outstanding first-mortgage bonds, as well as its preferred stock, to the same level.

Before closing this chapter, it is important to emphasize two other points.

First, in rating utility bonds in particular, Standard & Poor's strives strenuously to disregard short-term factors and concentrate on long-term trends. As Thomas Fendrich puts it: "Sometimes a company's fixed-charge coverage will decline to a point where it is below average even for the next rating down. But if, after talking with management and the regulatory bodies involved, we conclude that the situation is temporary and that positive long-term factors have not changed, we will maintain the current rating and look for improvement down the road."

Second, Standard & Poor's also strives strenuously to avoid issuing or changing a rating when a company is in the midst of an appeal for an increase in rates. Says Fendrich: "If a company's bond rating represents a borderline case and if the company has made a rate-increase appeal that seems near decision, we will do our very best to await the decision before rating the issue. After all, if a company's bonds were rated single-A yesterday, pushed down to triple-B today, and raised back to single-A tomorrow, who would be helped? Not the investor nor the company nor the consumer. The only result would be confusion and possibly speculation."

How Railroad and Airline Bonds Are Rated   7

It should be obvious to even the most inexperienced eye that the transportation industry is one of the most important in the country. It includes not only airlines and railroads, but also barge lines, private carriers, and truckers, all of which are vital to the distribution of the goods on which our society depends. Yet, despite the importance of this industry, the 1972 study by Salomon Brothers indicates that it accounts for only about 4 percent of the total amount of public corporate bonds outstanding, exclusive of equipment-trust certificates. There are several reasons why.

First, the airlines and, to a lesser extent, the railroads have not been in a position to borrow much money from the public long-term debt market in recent years. Many such companies have already put themselves too heavily into debt, and a number do not earn enough to cover their fixed charges.

Second, only two trucking companies currently have public long-term debt outstanding. Although truckers constantly replace their rolling stock, they tend to replace individual units of this stock about every seventh year. For this reason, they usually prefer to borrow on a secured short- and medium-term basis from banks rather than on a long-term basis from institutional and other kinds of investors.

Finally, no shipping companies have public long-term debt outstanding as that term is commonly thought of. Their only long-term debt consists of shipping mortgages that are guaranteed by the United States Government.

Thus we will study only the debt of airlines and railroads. Let us look at the two industries one at a time, beginning with the railroads.

There are 67 Class I lines in this country, which account for 99 percent of all railroad traffic, and a far larger number of Class II lines. To be categorized as a Class I line, a railroad must have at least $5 million in annual revenues.

Owing to several factors, including indenture limitations on the amount of new debt they may issue, few railroads have issued new bonds in recent years. Even so, virtually all of them still have public debt outstanding.

Most of the information they must give Standard & Poor's in order to have their debt rated is contained in their offering prospectuses. In addition, the investment advisory organization studies a thick form that the carriers file annually with the Interstate Commerce Commission. This form is known as R1 and contains a wealth of data on their operations.

In assaying railroad bonds and notes, Standard & Poor's looks at the same five factors it does in the case of most other kinds of corporate bonds and notes: indenture, asset protection, financial resources, future earning power, and management. Nevertheless, truly unusual attention is given to future earning power. You can understand why when you remember that many railroads' earnings have declined markedly in recent years. The rates the roads can charge are regulated by the ICC. In addition, airlines, truckers, and other carriers have made heavy inroads into their markets.

Because of the unusual importance of the railroads' estimated future earning power, Standard & Poor's places heavy emphasis on their coverage of fixed charges and their other statistical ratios. As we have seen, such ratios can be very important in rating most other kinds of bonds. But, according to Dominick G. Di Palma, a Standard & Poor's consultant who once oversaw its ratings of railroad and other corporate issues, "In the case of railroads, the fixed-charge coverage and other statistical ratios are unusually important."

Before studying these ratios—and, of course, the other factors that go into rating railroad bonds and notes—let us pause briefly to look at a

How Railroad and Airline Bonds Are Rated

special kind of debt issue that these carriers sell. It is known as an equipment-trust certificate and is structured to mature serially every 6 or 12 months over a 15-year period.

The proceeds from the sale of such certificates are used to purchase locomotives, freight cars, and other rolling stock. The equipment itself serves as collateral for the debt, and it invariably is insured or otherwise protected against fire, vandalism, and other casualties. Obviously, such stock is vital to the railroads' operations, and commonly it is highly marketable.

As a result, the certificates are considered safer than other kinds of railroad bonds. Because of the importance of rolling stock and because of its marketability, the railroads simply cannot afford not to pay interest on and retire their certificates as they mature. In fact, no equipment-trust certificate has ever been permanently defaulted on. During the Great Depression, the Florida East Coast Railroad once had to delay interest payments on its certificates, but payments, including payment of bank interest, were resumed within less than 1 year.

It is true that, in rating such certificates, Standard & Poor's looks at the same factors it looks at in other railroad bonds. But presuming everything else is in reasonable order, it is concerned as much as anything else with the carriers' fixed-charge coverages, plus the amounts due on certificates maturing in one year.

For a certificate to be rated single-A, its issuer's combined coverages, before allowance for depreciation, should ordinarily exceed the debt service requirements on its equipment at least one and one-quarter times; to be rated double-A, from one and three-quarters to two and one-quarter times; and to be rated triple-A, by a much higher margin. Despite these requirements, virtually all railroad equipment-trust certificates carry a rating of at least A or A−.

Although we have looked at these certificates very briefly, keep in mind that they play a very important role in railroads' financing. Thus at the end of one recent year, all the nation's railroads combined had $4.6 billion of equipment-trust certificates outstanding as against $4.1 billion of other kinds of long-term debt.

Now let us turn to other railroad bonds. Most are mortgage bonds rather than debentures.

In studying indentures, Standard & Poor's looks for most of the same things it looks for in the indentures for other kinds of bonds. It wants the railroads to promise not to issue debt senior to the debt in question. Also, it suggests that the carriers establish strong sinking funds, which will serve to retire a large portion of the debt before it matures.

It is worth noting that in recent years some railroads have sold collateral-trust bonds secured by bonds of issues already authorized. Because the latter issues were almost invariably selling for considerably less than their face value, the carriers were required to pledge additional bonds worth at least one and one-half times the value of the bonds authorized.

Standard & Poor's spends much less time studying a railroad's asset protection than you might think. As Dominick Di Palma explains: "In general, a railroad's property is worth only what it can earn. The rare exceptions involve railroads so vital to a given area that this necessity in and of itself gives their property worth."

So far as asset-protection ratios go, Standard & Poor's studies only one and gives it only minor weight in rating railroad bonds. The ratio relates a railroad's debt to its total capitalization.

For a line's principal bond issue to be a candidate for a rating of single-A, the debt should not ordinarily exceed 35 percent of capitalization. To be a candidate for an even higher rating, the debt should not exceed 25 percent of capitalization.

What about financial resources? In checking internal resources, Standard & Poor's is interested in two key ratios.

One relates the railroad's working capital to all its interest charges. As a rule, the investment advisory organization likes working capital to be at least one and one-half times as great as annual interest charges.

The other ratio pertains to cash flow and relates net income, plus depreciation, plus deferred taxes, plus noncash items, to all capital expenditures the railroad makes, all repayments of maturing equipment-trust certificates, and all sinking fund payments. If you look at the industry as a whole, you will find that its cash flow ratios roam all over the map.

Nonetheless, for a railroad's bond to be a candidate for a single-A rating, Standard & Poor's prefers that its net operating income and other earnings, plus noncash items, exceed its expenditures at least one and one-half times; for a double-A rating, two times; and for a triple-A rating, three times. Very few railroads meet the final requirement.

Yet, just as in the case of other kinds of bonds, these guidelines are not sacrosanct. Strengths or weaknesses in other areas can cause a railroad bond to be rated higher or lower than its working capital and cash flow ratios might seem to warrant.

How Railroad and Airline Bonds Are Rated 59

So far as external resources go, Standard & Poor's pays a great deal of attention to a railroad's bank relationships. Although very few roads borrow substantial sums from banks on a medium- or long-term basis, some establish good bank lines to support the issuance of commercial paper.

Standard & Poor's also pays considerable attention to any income a railroad receives from sources other than its own operations. Thus some lines own real estate, oil and gas subsidiaries, and other income-producing assets. Obviously, these assets can add considerably to their earnings. Indeed, in 1974, they accounted for 33 percent of the total earnings available for payment of the industry's fixed charges. Thus it should be self-evident that Standard & Poor's asks: What outside income does a railroad have? How stable is this income? What proportion of the line's total earnings does it provide?

Let us now turn to future earning power, the most important of all the factors that Standard & Poor's considers in weighing railroad bonds. As you can guess, a host of matters come into play.

First is the nature of the territory a given railroad serves. Are the territory's raw materials likely to vanish over a period of years, or have they become vital to the economy, as has coal ever since the energy crisis erupted? What kind of competition does the railroad face from airlines, truckers, and other methods of transportation? To what extent do the latter's rates differ from the railroad's rates?

Second is the freight tonnage the line carries. Standard & Poor's wants to know the principal kinds of tonnage the line transports, the breakdown of this tonnage according to revenue dollar, the trend in the amount of the tonnage over a 10-year period, and the trend in ton-miles over the same length of time.

In addition, the investment advisory organization is interested in the railroad's revenues as a percentage of its region's railroad revenues over the last 10 years, in its revenues as a percentage of national railroad revenues over the same period, and in its net operating income as a percentage of the total net operating income of Class I lines. Standard & Poor's compares all these figures against the railroad's past record and both the current and past records of other railroads.

On top of all this, Standard & Poor's looks at three important ratios. They provide good insight into the railroad's efficiency. The first and most important is the so-called operating ratio. It relates all of the railroad's expenses, before taxes, to its gross revenues. The second is known as the transportation ratio. It relates all of the railroad's direct operating costs, such as wages and other overhead, to its gross revenues. The third is called the maintenance ratio. It relates the line's maintenance costs, including depreciation, to gross revenues.

Di Palma says that a good operating ratio would show that the railroad's operating expenses amounted to no more than 78 percent of its gross revenues. Such a ratio would qualify the railroad's bonds for a double-A rating, other things being equal.

As usual, this guideline is not applied rigidly. It can be and sometimes is outweighed by other factors, either favorable or unfavorable. Besides, Standard & Poor's is interested in the 10-year trend of this and the other ratios, as it is in the case of most of the other factors pertaining to a railroad's earnings, such as freight tonnage carried and revenues as a percentage of regional and national railroad revenues.

One other figure helps the investment advisory organization gage a railroad's efficiency. This figure indicates the gross ton miles a line carries per each freight hour its trains run. Standard & Poor's multiplies this figure by the time the average haul takes and divides the result by the number of freight train miles the line runs. It then compares the end result with the figures for past years and with comparable figures for other railroads.

Dividend payouts are also taken into account. A few railroads pay out as much as 60 percent of their net income. But Standard & Poor's considers this ratio high.

The fact that railroads are regulated by the ICC must also be considered. Di Palma says the regulatory agency tends to treat all railroads alike. Even so, it has been slow to allow carriers to abandon unprofitable lines and reportedly been both slow and tough in granting adequate rate increases. Obviously, its hard-nosed stance has sometimes helped put many railroads in something of a financial bind.

Assessing railroad company managements poses special problems. On the one hand, railroad managers as a group are considered vastly superior to any we have known in the past. On the other hand, the hands of some railroad managers are largely tied. There is just not a great deal that they can do about some of their problems. Often this is because they cannot obtain timely and effective rate relief.

All this does not mean, of course, that the investment advisory organization pays no attention to railroad managements. In fact, it is particularly interested in a management's past and future projections of business activity. A look at past projections, compared with what actu-

How Railroad and Airline Bonds Are Rated

ally happened, tells a great deal about management's foresight and ability to plan. A look at future projections tells a great deal about where it wants to take its line. Says Di Palma:

A railroad's future will depend on its ability to finance its capital needs, as well as on high levels of traffic, greater operating efficiencies, lessened competition, and faster rate decisions to offset escalating costs. But other factors will also play a role. Is the railroad constructing or leasing custom-built equipment? Is it making greater use of containers for shipping purposes? Is it tailoring its services and its rates to the needs of shippers? And is it putting its yards under more efficient computer control? Answers to questions like these help differentiate good managements from mediocre ones.

Now let's see how Standard & Poor's recently rated a railroad bond. Burlington Northern owns the largest railroad system in the country. Early in 1974 it issued $60 million of 25-year consolidated mortgage bonds. As collateral, it pledged some bonds it had already authorized, plus specific property liens.

The company's revenues had climbed nearly 12 percent in the latest annual reporting period. But because of matters largely beyond its control, its net operating income had risen only about 2 percent, and its fixed-charge coverage was not as good as it once had been. Said Standard & Poor's:

Although Burlington Northern's fixed-charge coverage has not returned to pre-1970 levels, it has nevertheless shown continued improvement since 1970. At the same time, the outlook for railroad operations continues to be good in the light of the fuel-short U.S. economy, while increasing amounts of income are being provided by nonrail activities in lumber, coal, iron, and oil and gas. In view of the gradually strengthening fixed-charge coverage, the good lien position, and the promising outlook for both the rail and nonrail areas, we are maintaining a single-A rating on these bonds.

Let us now turn to airlines, which we can look at much more briefly. Four hard facts indicate why. First, no major domestic carrier has issued any public long-term debt in some time, aside from equipment-trust certificates and convertible subordinated debentures. Second, little of the major carriers' debt already outstanding bears a rating higher than triple-B. Third, many major carriers are in serious financial difficulties. Finally, there is an important drive afoot to deregulate the industry.

The last fact may be the most important of all. The Ford Administration is spearheading the move to deregulate the airlines, and the Civil

Aeronautics Board has already taken some steps to this end. Furthermore, the deregulation movement has the support of Senator Edward M. Kennedy, the influential Massachusetts Democrat.

Interestingly, the drive is opposed by most of the industry. Its executives fear that deregulation would cause a tremendous shakeout. Says a former chairman of the CAB who is now a lawyer for Pan American: "If we are deregulated, there would be only three or four survivors among the big 10 domestic carriers. The rest would go under."

The real point is, as this is written in late 1975, the whole situation surrounding the airlines is in flux. No one knows whether there will be total or near-total deregulation and, if there is, what the precise effect will be.

Nonetheless, Standard & Poor's has rated new issues of airline bonds in the past, and no doubt it will do so again when the major carriers are in a position to issue such. Furthermore, it requires the kind of information you would expect: detailed income statements and balance sheets, further financial data reaching at least 5 years into the past, projections of probably performance several years into the future, and so forth. Also, it looks at the same factors it looks at in other kinds of bonds.

Like the railroads, the airlines sometimes issue equipment-trust certificates, but these certificates play a far less significant role in their long-term financing than they do in the case of the railroads. Even so, Standard & Poor's rates these certificates in the same fashion that it rates regular airline bonds, regarding them as senior secured debt. And it considers them slightly safer than other senior debt.

The reason that it does not regard them as significantly safer, as it is inclined to do in the case of railroad equipment-trust certificates, is that planes purchased with the proceeds from the sale of certificates are not necessarily as marketable as are railroad cars. "Whether the planes are marketable," says Jerome J. Corcoran, an analyst, "depends on two factors. One is whether the economy is in a recession. In other words, the planes tend to be very marketable in good times, much less so in bad. The other factor is the kind of plane involved. Some of the big planes are very hard to sell in any kind of economic climate."

In evaluating regular long-term airline debt, Standard & Poor's looks for most of the same factors in indentures it looks for in the case of other kinds of bonds. Thus it wants an airline to promise that it will not issue any debt senior to the debt in question. It also wants the airline to promise not to issue any further debt unless its assets exceed its debt by a certain margin, commonly by at least two to one. Also, it prefers that the line retire its debt by means of a sinking fund.

In studying asset protection, Standard & Poor's looks at least a half-dozen ratios, capitalizing all leases in the process. These ratios include net plant assets to debt, net tangible assets to debt, working capital to debt, and debt to capitalization.

The most important, however, are cash flow to debt and total liabilities to stockholders' equity. In the first instance, Standard & Poor's prefers that cash flow equals or approaches 50 percent of debt. In the second, it prefers that liabilities not exceed stockholders' equity by more than two to one. Airlines with such ratios are candidates for at least single-A ratings, other things being equal.

One of an airline's strongest financial resources is a market that holds up reasonably well in good times and bad. Another is the nature of its planes and how they are depreciated. In general Standard & Poor's likes them to be depreciated as rapidly as possible, say within 10 to 14 years.

Today banks constitute one of an airline's very few external financial resources. Thus Standard & Poor's wants to know: To how many banks does a given airline have access? Is this access secured? For how long a period?

A carrier's staying power is an important factor in assessing its probable future earnings. As Jerome Corcoran explains: "United Airlines runs in and out of profitability. But it is the leader of its industry and has a huge system, plus good cash flow and a sizable cash position. So we believe that it will do relatively well over the long term, no matter how poorly it may do in a given year."

Another important factor is how a line's average passenger load compares with its break-even passenger load. Generally, the industry suffers from overcapacity.

Labor relations also play a key role in the success of an airline. Says Corcoran: "Some airlines maintain much better labor relations than others. This is important because a single union has sometimes shut down an entire airline for months. The loss of revenue in such a situation is bad enough. What's worse is that the airline often loses some share of its market."

Standard & Poor's also studies several ratios that are important indicators of an airline's economic health. One of the most significant is the number of employees a carrier has in relation to its total revenues.

Some lines have many more employees than others, which is not a good sign, other things being equal.

As you can guess, the investment advisory organization also checks an airline's fixed-charge coverage before giving its debt a rating. In general, for the debt to receive a rating of triple-B, its coverage should be better than two to one after taxes—and at least one and three-quarters to one if rental fees are included. For the debt to receive a single-A rating, coverage should be at least three times interest.

Dividends and taxes by contrast are given short shrift. Few lines pay much in the way of dividends, and most are taxed at a low rate. Says Corcoran:

> When we turn to management the first thing we want to know is how aware it is of its problems and what it is doing to solve them. It's true, of course, that some problems are regulation-related and that management can do nothing about them. Yet others are not.
>
> For example, some airlines have much lower costs in relation to sales than others do. And this is important because the CAB ties rate relief to the industry's average return on investment. Thus, when relief is granted, low-cost airlines fare much better than others.
>
> Despite this, some managements just seem to go along, hoping for the best. Ultimately, they look to government to solve all of their problems. Others do not.
>
> In any case we certainly want to know an airline's future financial plans. We also want to know its contingency plans in case earnings fall off—for example, how it would reduce its costs. And we want to know the reverse—how it would go about adding passenger capacity if the need arose.

But over the whole situation, as we have seen, hangs the threat—or salvation—of deregulation. Says Corcoran: "Frankly, we don't know what will happen. Something must because the industry is in trouble. Even so, we cannot overlook the fact that deregulation would benefit some airlines and hurt others."

How Bank Holding Company Bonds Are Rated   8

Standard & Poor's has rated bank holding companies' commercial paper since 1970 and their long-term debt and preferred stocks since October 1974. These holding companies may own not only banks but also other subsidiaries engaged in activities like commercial and consumer financing, leasing, factoring, and mortgage financing. In this connection it is important to understand that Standard & Poor's does not rate the securities issued by banks, but only those issued by bank holding companies.

Norman Johnson, who is a manager in Standard & Poor's corporate finance department and in charge of its bank holding company ratings, estimates that at the present time there are 200 such companies with assets of over $500 million apiece. He says the overwhelming majority of the larger of these companies have long-term debt outstanding, some of it privately placed.

Why do such companies issue debt? In recent years many of them have been unable to generate and retain sufficient capital internally to meet their needs. As a result, they have had to resort to the capital markets, largely the debt markets.

Some might have preferred to issue equity rather than debt, yet in 1974 and 1975 at least the stock market was not particularly receptive to the issuance of new bank stock. Many bank stocks were already selling for less than their book value. Issuance of further stock would have caused an undesirable dilution of the banks' earnings per share.

Standard & Poor's rates the securities of a bank holding company only on the request of the issuer. A company may reject the rating if it wishes. As of a recent date, the investment advisory organization had published ratings on the long-term debt of 15 such companies.* It had also rated a few privately placed issues.

To obtain a rating, a bank holding company must supply certain written information. This information includes a completed financial data questionnaire;† a complete set of audited financial statements for the past 5 years on both a fully consolidated and consolidating basis (the latter can be done by line of activity); the company's annual reports for the past 5 years; its recent interim financial statements; its most recent 10-K report; and a prospectus. Additional information and supporting data may be asked for as necessary.

In addition, Standard & Poor's needs to know the holding company's past and current status of operations, its future short-term and long-term financing requirements, and its plans to meet these requirements. Much of this information is obtained through interviews with top management.

Before seeing how Standard & Poor's uses this information, it is important to understand two basic points made by Norman Johnson.

"First," he says, "the rating of bank holding company debt is done less by the numbers than the debt of most other industries." He means that the statistical ratios—the assets to debt ratio, for example—that are so important to the rating of industrial and utility debt are considerably less important to the rating of bank holding company debt. In short, judgement plays an even greater role than usual.

Second, although Standard & Poor's always gives some weight to how

---

*A number of other companies applied for ratings, and Standard & Poor's studied their issues and, in some cases, even gave the issues preliminary ratings. But then, for one reason or another, the companies decided to postpone the issues.

†A financial data questionnaire is an elaborate, six-page form designed by Standard & Poor's to elicit detailed information from a bank holding company on its average assets, average liabilities, operating revenues and expenses, interest rates paid and earned, loan losses and reserves, and related matters. Questionnaires must be completed by both the bank holding company and its subsidiaries. Although Standard & Poor's does not rate long-term issues put out by banks, it must study their operations in order to properly evaluate their parents.

a particular company stacks up against comparable companies, such weight is of particular importance in the banking industry. The emphasis is on the word "comparable."

In other words, Standard & Poor's does not try to make direct comparisons between giant bank holding companies in big money centers like New York and Chicago and regional banks in, say, Iowa or Idaho. The scope and nature of regional bank holding companies is too different to permit extensive comparison with giant bank holding companies, although some limited comparisons are necessary, simply because both kinds of companies compete to some extent in the money markets.

To obtain a triple-A rating, a bank holding company's debt must meet eight standards. They are as follows:

1. The bank holding company must hold an important position in a significant banking market. Explains Johnson:

In banking, bigness has its definite advantages. A small or medium-sized regional bank holding company is more vulnerable to a local recession or other adversity than a large holding company that operates on a national or international basis. A smaller institution also often lacks clout in the marketplace.

During the summer of 1974, for example when tight money conditions prevailed, there was a flight of money, including both certificates of deposit and commercial paper, from regional institutions to the large bank holding companies, mainly those in New York City. In general this flight was not caused by problems at the regional institutions, but by the mystique of the giant bank holding company, a mystique that especially appealed to investors during that period. Obviously, this type of behavior has a definite impact on a company's assets, liquidity, and earnings.

2. The holding company must be soundly capitalized in relation to the nature of its operations.

Among other things, Standard & Poor's ascertains whether the holding company is financing its long-term assets with short-term debt, which has its drawbacks, and the extent to which the company is using the proceeds from debt to make equity investments in its subsidiaries. It also studies the kind of lending the holding company's subsidiaries are doing and the risks involved.

3. The company's debt (amount, maturity, and usage) should be sound in relation to its total capitalization.

An accepted yardstick for banks is that debt should not exceed 35 to 50 percent of equity (common and preferred stock, plus surplus, undivided profits, and contingency reserves). But this ratio can be adjusted upward by a holding company that has nonbank subsidiaries. The reason is that most nonbank subsidiaries that lend money can be much more highly leveraged in terms of long-term debt to equity than a bank and still have satisfactory debt ratios.

4. The holding company's earnings should be sufficient in amount and growth in relation to the amount of and growth in its assets.

Among other things, Standard & Poor's is interested in the diversity, quality, and volatility of the company's earnings, including those emanating from its nonbank subsidiaries, as well as in the mix of its assets. Many larger institutions do a lot of trading in money-market instruments like federal funds and commercial paper and do interbank lending in the form of redeposits. The net return from these activities is usually low, which, of course, puts some damper on earnings as a percentage of total assets. As a result, the makeup of the company's assets must be analyzed before it can be determined how satisfactory the level of earnings on assets is.

5. The company's asset and liability structure should be in balance and easily manageable.

A key question involves the interest-rate sensitivity of assets as compared to liabilities. If the interest earned on assets can move upward and downward in conjunction with the cost of lendable funds, then the holding company's net interest margin will remain relatively constant. And changes in interest rates will have minimal impact on its earnings.

Institutions that have an imbalance in their interest-sensitive assets and liabilities, on the other hand, are buffeted by changes in interest rates, and their earnings tend to be volatile. During 1974, for example, when high interest rates generally prevailed, institutions that had sizable amounts of fixed-rate assets supported by liabilities that were sensitive to changes in interest rates suffered severe declines in earnings.

6. Both the holding company and its subsidiaries should have sound loan-loss reserves relative to their assets, plus favorable loss records.

There is a rule of thumb that a bank's valuation reserve should equal one percent of its outstanding loans. But this rule is not magic. The key questions are, How do the company's reserve and its loss record compare with what they have been in the past? What is the current condition of its loan portfolio?

How Bank Holding Company Bonds Are Rated

The latter is perhaps the more important of the two questions. Yet it does not always lend itself to easy answer. Because different kinds of lending carry different kinds of risks, a bank with a loss record of 0.20 percent of average loans may actually have a better record than one whose loss record is 0.10 percent.

7. The quality and liquidity of the company's assets should be more than satisfactory in relation to its liabilities.

In this case Standard & Poor's compares the mix of the company's assets to the mix of its liabilities. There are several factors to be considered. One is how sensitive both assets and liabilities are to interest rates. Another is how volatile both assets and liabilities are. A third involves the quality of the assets in comparison with the quality of the company's equity and reserves. In all these matters, comparisons are made against the company's past record and the current and past records of comparable companies.

8. The quality and reliability of management should be above question.

To have its debt qualify for a triple-B—or possibly higher—rating, a bank holding company must meet essentially the same criteria as cited above, but to a lesser degree. Thus the company does not have to be a major factor in a major money center. But the scope of its operations and its competitive position should be strong enough to indicate that it will remain reasonably profitable. The amount, maturity, and usage of its debt may not be in ideal proportion to its capitalization, but the company should be able to adequately service the debt. Its earnings should show promise of future growth, and its loss record and loss reserve should be satisfactory.

Before Standard & Poor's began rating bank holding company debt, it devised a computerized data base for the industry, specifically oriented to debt as opposed to equity analysis. The data base was compiled from information supplied by 65 bank holding companies. It contains slightly more than 100 ratios, including median figures and decile scores, for the bank holding companies on a fully consolidated basis and also for their subsidiary banks. A few parent-company only ratios are also included.

The ratios are pertinent enough so that it is worth listing them in full, but it is important to emphasize that, even as this book is being written, the list is being revised, with some being dropped and others added.

How Corporate and Municipal Debt is Rated

Nonetheless, most are being retained, and the list will give you a good idea of the kind and depth of information Standard & Poor's seeks. The ratios are as follows:

Operating Results

Net operating income as it relates to such income for the preceding year;* net operating income as a percentage of average income plus reserves for the most recent year; net average income as a percentage of average equity plus reserves plus capital debt for the most recent year; net operating income as a percentage of gross earning assets for the most recent year;† net operating income as a percentage of basic earning assets for the most recent year;‡ the effective tax rate for the most recent year; the muni-max tax rate for the most recent year;§ muni-adjusted taxable income in thousands of dollars per employee for the most recent year; **the same figure for 5 years ago.

Earning Asset Ratios

Total assets as a percentage of gross earning assets for the most recent year; the same figure for 5 years ago; basic earning assets as a percentage of gross earning assets for the most recent year; the same figure for 5 years ago; the trading account as a percentage of gross earning assets for the most recent year; the same figure for 5 years ago; temporary investments as a percentage of gross earning assets for the most recent year; the same figure for 5 years ago; loans as a percentage of gross earning assets for the most recent year; the same figure for 5 years ago; market-sensitive liabilities as a percentage of gross earning assets for the most recent year; the same figure for 5 years ago; consumer time deposits as a percentage of gross earning assets for the most recent year;

*This figure is computed for each of the past 5 years.
†Gross earnings include loans, investments, federal funds sold, repurchase agreements, and certificates of deposit, both domestic and international.
‡Basic earnings assets constitute loans and investments.
§The muni-max tax rate represents the company's income tax liability incurred against pretax net income, less income on tax-free securities.
**Muni-adjusted taxable income is reported pretax income, adjusted upward to reflect tax-equivalent income on tax-free securities.

How Bank Holding Company Bonds Are Rated

the same figure for 5 years ago; overhead as a percentage of gross earning assets for the most recent year; the same figure for 5 years ago; overhead less trust revenues as a percentage of gross earning assets; the same figure for 5 years ago; interest expense less trading account interest income as a percentage of gross earning assets for the most recent year; the same figure for 5 years ago; the change in gross earning assets between the most recent year and the prior year; the change in gross earning assets between the most recent year and 5 years ago; the change in basic earning assets between the most recent year and 5 years ago; the change in loans between the most recent year and the prior year; the change in loans between the most recent year and 5 years ago; the change in demand deposits between the most recent year and 5 years ago; the change in consumer time deposits between the most recent year and 5 years ago; the change in market-sensitive liabilities between the most recent year and the prior year; the change in market-sensitive liabilities between the most recent year and 5 years ago; the loan yield in the most recent year; the loan yield 5 years ago; the investment security yield in the most recent year; the investment security yield 5 years ago; the gross earning assets in the most recent year; the same figure for 5 years ago; interest expense as a percentage of gross earning assets in the most recent year; the same figure for 5 years ago; the net yield margin in the most recent year; the same figure for 5 years ago; temporary investments as a percentage of market-sensitive liabilities in the most recent year; the same figure for 5 years ago.

Loss Ratios

The loan-loss reserve as a percentage of loans for the most recent year; the valuation portion of the loan-loss reserve as a percentage of loans for the most recent year;* net loan charge-offs as a percentage of loans for the most recent year; loan-loss provisions as a percentage of loans for the most recent year; average net charge-offs as a percentage of loans over the past 5 years; the valuation portion of the loan-loss reserve as a percentage of average net charge-offs over the past 5 years.

*The valuation reserve is that portion of the reserve for loan losses that has passed through the income statement. It is the only portion of the reserve to which loan losses can be charged.

Expense Ratios

The change in overhead between the most recent year and 5 years ago; the change in staff expense between the most recent year and 5 years ago; staff expense as a percentage of overhead for the most recent year; the same figure for 5 years ago; muni-adjusted taxable income as a percentage of overhead for the most recent year; the same figure for 5 years ago.

Capital Ratios

Stock equity plus reserves as a percentage of gross earning assets for the most recent year; the same figure for 5 years ago; stock equity less twice the amount of trust revenues as a percentage of gross earning assets for the most recent year; the same figure for 5 years ago; stock equity plus reserves plus capital debt as a percentage of gross earning assets for the most recent year; the same figure for 5 years ago; stock equity plus reserves as a percentage of loans for the most recent year; the same figure for 5 years ago; long-term debt as a percentage of long-term debt plus equity plus reserves for the most recent year; the same figure for 5 years ago; net capital as a percentage of gross earning assets for the most recent year.

Pretax Interest Coverages

Pretax interest coverage on long-term borrowings for the most recent year; for the year before that; for 5 years ago; on all borrowings for the most recent year; for the year before that; for 5 years ago.

Bank/Consolidated Holding Company Ratios

Bank net operating income as a percentage of the consolidated holding company's net operating income for the most recent year; for the year before that; for 5 years ago; bank equity as a percentage of the consolidated holding company's equity for the most recent year; for the year before that; for 5 years ago; bank total assets as a percentage of the

How Bank Holding Company Bonds Are Rated

consolidated holding company's total assets for the most recent year; for the year before that; for 5 years ago.

Ratios for the Parent Company Only

The current ratio for the most recent year; the same ratio for the year before that; current liabilities as a percentage of total liabilities for the most recent year; the same figure for the year before that; long-term senior debt as a percentage of long-term debt plus net worth for the most recent year; the same figure for the year before that; total liabilities as a percentage of net worth for the most recent year; the same figure for the year before that; the double leverage ratio for the most recent year;* the same figure for the year before that; double leverage payback for the most recent year;† the same figure for the year before that; net tangible assets as a percentage of senior debt for the most recent year; the same figure for the year before that; net tangible assets as a percentage of total debt for the most recent year; the same figure for the year before that; after-tax interest coverage for the most recent year; the same figure for the year before that; pretax interest coverage for the most recent year; the same figure for the year before that.

That is a long list of statistical ratios, but by looking at so many Standard & Poor's reduces the amount of time it takes to make an initial analysis of a company and to get quickly at the major items of actual or potential concern. Thus the major purpose of some ratios is to point up the most pertinent characteristics of a bank.

Although Standard & Poor's computes all these ratios in relation to any bank holding company debt it rates, it does not necessarily employ all of them in assessing the company's bonds. In fact, it often concentrates much of its attention on only seven or eight ratios, which may differ from company to company. This is because some of the ratios of a particular company may be markedly out of line with those of comparable companies or because of the nature of the company's business.

There are still other matters that Standard & Poor's looks into. These fall into the same general categories used in the rating of other corporate bonds—indenture, asset protection, and so forth.

---

*The double leverage ratio equals the holding company's equity investment in its subsidiaries as a percentage of its own net worth.

††Double leverage payback indicates the number of years required for the current year's income, exclusive of securities transactions, to equal the excess of the holding company's equity investments in its subsidiaries over its own net worth.

In general an indenture plays a smaller role in the rating of bank holding company debt than it does in the rating of the debt of companies in other industries. To cite one example, Standard & Poor's is less concerned than it ordinarily would be that the issuing company establish a sinking fund, assuming that the debt is not truly of a long-term nature. Because of regulatory considerations, most bank holding company debt must have an original maturity of at least 7 years. But because much of the debt sold recently has had a maturity of 8 to 10 years, sinking funds have not been practical.

Nor is Standard & Poor's overly concerned with the ratio between the holding company's actual cash flow and its debt. More important is the amount of potential cash flow, the major source of which involves dividends sent from the subsidiaries to the holding company.

Explains Johnson: "We look at the relationship of the total earnings of the subsidiaries, the dividends paid to the parent, the dividends paid to shareholders, and the capital requirements of the company. This analysis gives us a good feel for how much cash flow is really available for debt service."

In this connection, in a great many cases a dividend-payout ratio of 50 percent would be considered very high, at least in a year in which earnings were normal. Many holding companies pay out about 35 percent, and the overall trend is toward an even lower percentage.

Again, Standard & Poor's does not direct much attention to the ratio between the holding company's assets and its debt. It is more interested in the ratio between its debt and its equity. As we have seen, debt should not ordinarily exceed 50 percent of equity, but this ratio does not necessarily hold true in the case of a holding company with considerable nonbank activities. It must also be tempered in accordance with how highly the company's subsidiaries are leveraged and with the subsidiaries' profitability.

Standard & Poor's studies a ratio known in the banking industry as the double leverage ratio. This ratio reflects the amount of equity the holding company has invested in its subsidiaries in relation to its own net worth.

Double leverage usually arises this way: First, a holding company, whose assets are its equity holdings in its subsidiaries, issues long-term debt, thus leveraging up on its equity. Then the company uses the proceeds from the debt to make additional equity investments in its subsidiaries, whereupon the subsidiaries themselves issue debt based

How Bank Holding Company Bonds Are Rated

on their stated equity account. This process of using debt to support additional debt is referred to as double leverage. One possible result is that the combined capitalization of the subsidiaries may be greater than that of their parent.

This is not necessarily bad if the excess is modest, if the quality of assets is good, and if the subsidiaries all have satisfactory earnings. It is a cause for worry, however, if the excess is substantial and, more important, if the subsidiaries' earnings are poor or erratic. In the latter case the subsidiaries may not be able to provide the holding company with as much cash flow as expected.

Yet another problem can arise when the proceeds from holding company debt is used to make equity investments in bank subsidiaries. Even if the subsidiaries' earnings are satisfactory, the subsidiaries may not be able to pay sufficient dividends to enable the parent to service its own debt, especially if there is a large amount of debt to be paid off. A dividend limitation applies to many banks, in that the dividends they may pay in any one year are limited to that year's earnings, plus the retained earnings of the prior 2 years. Bank regulators can grant exceptions to this restriction on a case-by-case basis, but there is no guarantee that they will do so.

In addition, bank regulators can stop the payment of dividends if in their opinion the payment would amount to unsound banking practice. It seems that the regulators have used this power sparingly, at least with the larger bank holding companies. Yet an uncertainty about dividend-paying ability persists, and Standard & Poor's feels it must consider this problem in the rating process.

A key item in an evaluation of a bank holding company is the quality and liquidity of the loan portfolio, but determining this is easier said than done. The loan-loss record of recent years may be misleading. Bank management may have purposely made some high-risk loans, a few of which resulted in charge-offs. Thus an important consideration is whether such loans were priced properly to compensate for the risks taken. Determining whether this was the case is a matter of judgement.

Standard & Poor's may also ask for a breakdown of the loan-loss record over a period of time to ascertain whether most of the losses were in the commercial, consumer, or some other area and whether the company has been keeping on top of them. Observes Johnson: "Some companies have very sophisticated systems for monitoring losses. Others fly by the seat of their pants."

The liquidity of the current portfolio is also looked into. Different types of loans, of course, have different liquidity considerations. Basically, Standard & Poor's wants to know whether a sizable number of borrowers are constantly rolling over their loans and thus limiting the real liquidity of the bank's loan portfolio.

Another area that is checked is the scope of the holding company's activities. Does the bank have what can be described as a usual mix of business on both sides of the balance sheet? Or has it specialized in certain functions to the exclusion of others? If the organization has an unusual balance, is it due to design, happenstance, or an inability to get into certain banking markets?

In estimating a holding company's future earning power, Standard & Poor's looks first at the balance sheet and earnings statement. If both look good, this usually indicates that the company will be able to raise money in the capital markets, no matter what the condition of those markets.

The investment advisory organization is also interested in the company's projections of its earnings several years into the future. If earnings are expected to increase much faster than assets, Standard & Poor's wants to know why.

Johnson does not equate projections with predictions. But he stresses that projections help a company plan its future and anticipate changes.

Tax practices also play a role in Standard & Poor's assessment. Some companies pay very little in taxes. "We know that this is probably not by design," Johnson observes. "The company has probably loaded up heavily on tax-exempt municipal bonds. Yet it might have earned more from taxable bonds."

Standard & Poor's also casts an eye on the company's internal financial controls. This can be particularly important if the company does a lot of trading in foreign currencies. What monetary and other limits has it placed on such trading? How does it make sure its traders observe these limits? How often does it check up? It was a failure in just this area that contributed to the collapse of Franklin National Bank in 1974.

The company's fixed-charge coverage ratio is considered less important than it would be in another kind of corporation. Banks are in the interest-differential business. The result, as we have seen, is that Standard & Poor's is much more concerned with whether a company maintains approximately the same spread between the interest it pays its depositors and the interest it charges its borrowers under any and all conditions.

How Bank Holding Company Bonds Are Rated 77

Management is asked most of the same questions that other corporate managements are asked. Johnson indicates that he is particularly concerned with the company's forward planning, with what it wants to do differently and why. Companies that do little or no forward planning are suspect.

Standard & Poor's also looks into the management-succession program. "On this matter," says Johnson, "there are no right and wrong answers. But we try to find out about any new men brought into upper management ranks and why it was necessary to bring them in, about the impact on morale, and about any important executives who have been lost and why. A company that says it has never lost an important manager immediately raises the question: Just how good are your people? Does nobody else want them? Or are they very happy where they are?"

Most of what has been said thus far refers to a holding company and its banking subsidiaries. Most holding companies receive 95 percent or more of their assets and earnings from these subsidiaries, and it is logical that they have received most of the attention.

What about nonbank subsidiaries? The amount of attention they receive relates to their present and projected size, the activities they engage in, and the nature of the problems they face. In looking at these subsidiaries Standard & Poor's leans toward a building-block approach. One tenet of this approach is that nonbank subsidiaries should be capitalized in much the same fashion as similarly situated independent companies, although under some circumstances, as in a start-up operation, variations from the normal capitalization ratios can exist.

Now let us see how all these factors were applied recently to two bank holding companies.

J.P. Morgan & Co. owns three subsidiaries. Far and away the most important is Morgan Guaranty Trust, which ranks as the sixth largest commercial bank in the country. In August 1975 the holding company registered $150 million of 7-year notes. Although it later withdrew this issue, the issue had already been rated by Standard & Poor's.

Said the investment advisory organization:

J.P. Morgan & Co. is an exceptionally well-managed bank holding company. The bank's capital ratios are substantially stronger than those of any of the other top 10 money-center banks, and its return on both assets and equity also exceeds that of any of the money-center banks. While asset quality is high as evidenced by a below-average level of loan charge-offs, the valuation portion of the loan-loss reserve, as a percentage of outstanding loans, is well above the average of the bank holding company industry. Accounting policies and controls appear conservative, and debt usage is moderate.

Not surprisingly, the issue received a rating of AAA.

Boatmen's Bancshares, Inc. is a multibank holding company and at the end of 1974 was the fifth largest such company in Missouri. It owns 13 banks in that state, the largest of which is The Boatmen's National Bank of St. Louis. In October 1975 the parent company sold $10 million of 8-year notes.

As Standard & Poor's saw it, the holding company had several points in its favor. For one thing, even though its banks were considerably smaller than the major institutions in St. Louis and Kansas City, it enjoyed a good market position in the major metropolitan areas of the state. To cite another example, it had good capital ratios.

On the other hand, the company had grown extremely rapidly in recent years, both through acquisition of other banks and through internal expansion. Although Standard & Poor's did not view this growth as necessarily cause for concern, it did view it as cause for uncertainty.

Concluded the rating agency:

Although the company's recent record of earnings has been good and profitability is at a more than satisfactory level, we feel a little more time is needed to fully evaluate all of the holding company's acquisitions of the past few years. Based on the foregoing, plus a fine management team and a reasonable usage of debt in the capital structure, we have assigned the rating of A to this issue of notes.

In sum then, rating bank debt is something of a curiosity. More than almost any other kind of company, a bank deals in figures. Naturally, Standard & Poor's studies these figures carefully, using more than 100 ratios to pinpoint their significance, yet its judgment plays an equal, if not a greater, role in the ratings it gives.

How Finance Bonds Are Rated   9

Thousands of finance companies dot this country. Most are small personal-loan companies that operate on the local level. They are, therefore, of no relevance to this chapter. Yet at least 200 other finance companies of varying size and nature borrow in the national debt markets. They include commercial finance companies, consumer finance firms, factors, leasing concerns, sales finance outfits, and various combinations of these and related businesses.

In certain important respects, rating these companies' debt differs from rating other corporations' debt. For one thing, to have their debt rated, they must be of a certain size. Specifically, they must have $25 million in equity capital or $35 million in capital funds. Also, statistical ratios are less important in rating the debt of finance companies than they are in rating many other kinds of debt. In this regard finance companies resemble banks and differ from industrial concerns and utilities. There are several reasons for this. Explains Edward C. Bray, assistant to Standard & Poor's vice president for corporate finance:

Finance companies can change both their structure and the nature of their assets very rapidly, simply by going into new lines of business. Such companies are also more subject to both external and internal fraud than most other kinds of companies. Finally, the quality of their accounts receivable is at least as important as any statistical ratio that might be applied against them. In other words, a company may be only slightly leveraged. But if its accounts receivable are worth only 50 cents on the dollar, what good is the low leverage?

For some of the same reasons, only one finance company in the country currently has its long-term debt rated triple-A. It is a wholly owned subsidiary of Sears, Roebuck and owns only Sears' notes. Very obviously, this means that the debt issues of some other well-known and well-regarded finance companies carry lower ratings.

There are two reasons for this other than those cited. One is that although the ratings given such companies' bonds are long-term ratings, the companies' assets are subject to rapid, short-term change. The other is that the fortunes of such companies are usually tied very directly to changes in interest rates. In other words, depending on what interest rates do and what the various states allow finance companies to charge in interest, the companies' earnings may be very good or very poor in any given year.

The information Standard & Poor's requires from a finance company in order to rate its bonds or notes include a copy of the prospectus and indenture; long-form audits, when available, or other financial statements, covering the most recent 5 years; a Robert Morris questionnaire;* and a schedule of receivable liquidations.†

In addition, Standard & Poor's wants to know the company's reason for issuing debt, its future short-term and long-term financing needs, its plans for meeting these needs, and the current status of its operations. Much of this kind of information is obtained through talks with management.

In correlating this information, Standard & Poor's does not break it down into the categories it usually employs in rating bonds—indenture, asset protection, and so forth. Instead, it breaks it down into four other categories—portfolio, income protection, capital structure, and management.

The portfolio, of course, consists of the finance company's outstanding loans. The first question Standard & Poor's asks is whether the company's accounts receivable are worth what they are valued at on its books. In this connection accounting practices reveal a great deal.

---

*A Robert Morris questionnaire provides a breakdown of a finance company's accounts receivable on both the wholesale and retail level.

†This schedule shows what proportion of a company's accounts receivable are contractually due over varying periods of time and what its actual collection experience has been.

How Finance Bonds Are Rated

Other questions Standard & Poor's asks include the following: Is the company taking in income too rapidly? If so, its future earnings capacity will suffer.

Is it reporting its income on an accrual or a cash basis? If the former, it may be crediting itself with income that it will never receive.

Again, if it is on an accrual basis, at what point does it decide an account is delinquent and, therefore, stop crediting itself with income?

What constitutes payment anyway? Some companies regard only full, regular reimbursement of the money that is owed them as payment. Others regard partial payments or even payments of interest only as sufficient, at least for the time being, and, therefore, do not list such accounts as delinquent.

What is the company's charge-off policy—that is, at what point does it charge off a loan as uncollectible? Many do so after 6 months, some sooner, some later. The policy the company follows will, of course, affect its loss record and its asset quality.

Does the company report delinquent accounts on a recency or a contractual basis? In the first instance it reports them as delinquent only if a month or more has elapsed since the last payment was made. In the second it reports them as delinquent if at any time they are behind the terms of their original contracts by as little as 30 days.

Standard & Poor's much prefers the latter, more conservative method. The reason is simple. A customer of a finance company could be required to make 12 payments in a 12-month period. Under the recency method of reporting delinquent accounts, he could make only six payments and not be counted in arrears, provided he had made the latest payment within the last 30 days. Under the contractual method, he would be counted as 6 months in arrears.

Does the company impose extra charges when a customer is delinquent? Most finance companies are allowed to do this, and in such cases Standard & Poor's wants to know how successful they have been in collecting these additional charges.

What are the company's policies on extensions and rewrites of loans? Because almost all finance companies provide for such, Standard & Poor's is not concerned with the practice in and of itself, but it is concerned with what proportion of loans are extended or rewritten. A big proportion may indicate that something is wrong with the company's lending practices. Standard & Poor's is also concerned with what proportion of such loans involve little or no advance of additional cash. A high proportion may mean that the company is taking extraordinary steps to keep late payors off its delinquency list.

What controls does the company exercise over its loans? For example, can a branch office extend or rewrite a loan at will? If so, how often? If not, at what point must it obtain approval of a regional supervisor or the home office credit committee? And how often are the branch offices audited?

What is the company's loss record on loans? How does this compare with its past record and with the current records of comparable companies?

What is the company's reserve against losses? It should usually be larger than the company's peak annual loss in recent years and should ordinarily be one and one-half times as large as the most recent annual loss. In addition, it should cover a substantial amount of delinquent and other problem accounts.

Does the company require collateral? In consumer finance the company usually cannot sell collateral at a profit. This collateral merely gives the company a psychological advantage over the consumer. But in other fields, like commercial finance, collateral is very important. Thus it may consist of an assignment of all or part of the borrower's accounts receivable, raw materials, or finished goods. Standard & Poor's wants to know what the arrangement is.

How concentrated is the company's portfolio? Excessive concentration can take place in various ways—in the size of the geographic area served, in the type of customers served, in the kinds of loans the customers take out, or in the size of such loans. The more diversified a company is in any and all of these respects, the better able it is to weather a recession.

These, then, are the basic questions Standard & Poor's asks about a finance company's portfolio. In many cases there are no right and wrong answers. Much depends on the nature of the company involved and how it stacks up against its own past record and the current records of its competitors. Even so, it should be obvious that when delinquencies are always reported on a recency basis and when there are frequent rewrites or extensions of loans, above-average losses, and haphazard controls, the issuing company had better have everything else going for it if it hopes to obtain an investment-grade rating (triple-B or better) on its debt.

Income protection is the next important area Standard & Poor's looks at. Such protection boils down to the fixed-charge coverage that a finance company enjoys. Edward Bray says that to have its debt qualify for a rating of at least triple-B, the company should ordinarily earn enough to cover its fixed charges at least one and one-quarter times over.

Naturally, a better ratio is desirable. Unfortunately, however, finance companies tend to suffer from wide swings in the level of their coverage. One or more of three reasons is usually responsible: the amount of short-term debt the company has outstanding, the company's ability to adjust the amount of interest it charges in light of changing interest rates, and the general level of such rates. The wider the swings in the company's coverage over a period of time, the more closely Standard & Poor's looks at it. It is particularly interested in how quickly the company can adjust the amount of interest it charges.

The investment advisory organization also studies the quality of the company's earnings very carefully. In this connection it once again pays close attention to how the company takes in income, its level of losses, and its reserve against losses.

Obviously, the nature and mix of a company's business can also affect its earnings. Standard & Poor's is willing to accept a lower level of fixed-charge coverage from a firm that can demonstrate superior quality of operations and control over them. If the company has captive insurance operations, Standard & Poor's examines how much income it obtains from them in the form of commissions or dividends. Obviously, it is best if such income is forthcoming on a regular basis and at a reasonably stable level.

Capital structure is the third major area Standard & Poor's looks into in studying a finance company. Its study is largely, although not entirely, statistical.

One of the first ratios it looks at is the relation between the company's total debt and its equity—in other words, its degree of leverage. Says Bray:

> We have a found that even a good company whose leverage exceeds seven to one is likely to get into trouble. As a general rule, we prefer that leverage not exceed five and one-half to one, although this figure can be bent, depending on the nature, circumstances, and track record of a particular company.
>
> For example, a captive finance company can sometimes be leveraged by as much as seven to one, yet receive an even higher rating than a company with less leverage. This might be true if the captive could lean heavily on its parent.

Again, a captive company might successfully carry a greater amount of debt to equity than seven to one, provided its total amount of debt were relatively small in relation to its parent's resources.

Standard & Poor's also looks at the ratio between a finance company's senior (unsubordinated) debt and its capital funds (equity plus long-term subordinated debt). As a rule, it prefers that the ratio not exceed three and one-half to one.

In addition, the investment advisory organization checks the company's current liabilities in relation to its net receivables. What is an acceptable ratio depends on the nature of the company and the maturities in its portfolio. In the case of an equipment-leasing company, current liabilities should not amount to more than about 40 percent of receivables. In the case of a consumer loan company, they should not amount to more than 60 percent. In the case of a factoring concern, however, they may go as high as 70 percent.

The investment advisory organization also probes a company's relationships with its banks. These relationships are particularly important to a finance company because, unless it is very big, it is not always able to tap the nation's capital markets.

For this reason, Standard & Poor's looks not only at the company's total bank lines, but also at which banks it is using. Only a dozen or so banks are expert in lending to finance companies. Thus Standard & Poor's likes to make sure at least a few of these are included on the company's list, that their commitments are tested fairly regularly, and that they are kept well informed. Says Bray: "We always call a few banks to see if they are happy with their relations with the company in question and whether they are being kept informed of its operations and plans."

Standard & Poor's is also interested in the company's philosophy on these and related matters, such as the amount of short-term debt it is willing to carry in relation to long-term debt. In general the investment advisory organization likes to see long-term receivables financed by long-term debt, short-term receivables by short-term debt.

In this connection Bray cites an example of a company whose philosophy got it in serious trouble. The company did not want and did not have any long-term debt. This meant that all its liabilities were of a short-term nature. Because it had lots of cash and could ordinarily borrow more in the commercial paper market, the company was uncon-

How Finance Bonds Are Rated

cerned. But then interest rates shot up, and the commercial paper market was closed to all but the very best credit risks. For a while the company was at the mercy of its bankers. Obviously, this did not enhance its standing with Standard & Poor's.

Management is the final area Standard & Poor's looks at in assessing a finance company. As you can guess, it is interested in studying management's philosophy, capability, experience, maturity, and depth. These factors are unusually important in the case of a finance company, because its management is its only real tangible asset. The questions asked include:

Is the senior manager the controlling stockholder? This can be good or bad, depending on his attitude toward his business.

Does management have the ability to change with the times? In this connection some types of financing are proving increasingly more attractive than others.

Does management plan to expand and diversify? If so, does it have enough managers and controls in place to do the job? If the company plans to acquire nonfinancial organizations, Standard & Poor's is also concerned with how the company plans to finance them. Nonfinancial firms cannot ordinarily carry as much leverage as a finance company.

Whether it plans to expand or not, are its controls adequate and its reports to management complete and on time? Procedures for auditing branch offices are considered particularly important.

Does management use modern tools? Some consumer loan companies have computerized, multipurpose credit-scoring systems that do auditing and bookkeeping and report loan volumes, cash flow, and so forth on a daily basis. Other companies do not, or if they do, their systems are not totally effective.

It is important to understand that Standard & Poor's assessment of a finance company depends somewhat on whether it is a captive company. A captive company is in business primarily to finance its parent's sales, wholesale, retail, or both. General Motors Acceptance Corp., Ford Motor Credit, and Fruehauf Finance all fall in this category. In these cases Standard & Poor's is interested in four factors: the strength of the parent, the quality and quantity of the parent's investment in the captive, the nature of the operating agreement between the two, and the captive's portfolio and structure.

Naturally, the stronger the parent is, the better. But Standard & Poor's wants to ascertain how much support it could provide its captive in bad times, whether it would correct deficiencies, and whether this support would actually be forthcoming.

The quality and quantity of the parent's investment is looked at from several angles. How significant is the investment to the parent? If its captive defaulted, would this merely embarrass the parent or would it really sting? Has the parent advanced a lot of equity as permanent capital to the captive or merely put up debt that the captive will have to repay? Can the parent withdraw any part of its investment, or does it merely have call on part of the captive's earnings?

Many of these same questions are asked about the operating agreement. Standard & Poor's is particularly concerned with whether the parent has agreed to maintain ownership of the captive, with whether it has put some equity into it, and with whether it has imposed some limit on how much it will take out of it in dividends.

The investment advisory organization looks at the captive's portfolio and structure in the same way it would look at those of an independent finance company. Thus it studies the captive's receivables, its method of taking in income, its loan policies, and so forth.

Even when a finance company is not a captive, it may be a wholly owned subsidiary. General Electric Credit and Westinghouse Credit are examples. If the subsidiary is stronger than the parent, Standard & Poor's wants to be sure that the parent cannot abuse the relationship.

A case in point arose just a few years ago. Control Data bought Commercial Credit. Shortly thereafter, Commercial Credit issued a long-term bond. At the time, its parent was considered a good, but not an overwhelmingly good, credit risk. The two firms enjoyed a reasonable amount of intercompany transactions. But Standard & Poor's was concerned lest this amount grow to undue proportions. Thus with the concurrence of both companies and with Commercial Credit's underwriters, it urged that a clause be inserted in the indenture limiting the amount of intercompany business. As a result, if such business approaches the maximum percentage allowed, Commercial Credit must reduce its debt load. The point is, Commercial Credit's bondholders are protected against any important negative developments in the affairs of the parent.

Let us turn now to two recent examples of how Standard & Poor's rated the debt issues of finance companies.

C.I.T. Financial is a huge, widely diversified finance company engaged in business and consumer financing, banking, insurance, man-

How Finance Bonds Are Rated

ufacturing, and merchandising. In June 1975 it issued $150 million of 20-year debentures.

In 1974 its operating income had declined by nearly 3 percent, but this trend had then reversed itself in the first quarter of 1975. Furthermore, its long-term earnings record had been exceptional in that it had never before declined in a period exceeding two decades. Its loss record had also been consistently better than average, and its net tangible assets equaled nearly 132 percent of its senior debt. Standard & Poor's said the firm's record, plus its widely diversified portfolio, conservative capital structure, and well-qualified management, warranted a double-A rating for its debentures.

About the same time, General Electric Credit issued $200 million worth of medium-term notes. This firm is also big and widely diversified and engaged in consumer, commercial, and industrial financing.

In recent quarters the company had suffered from a rising rash of delinquent payments and net losses, as had most of the rest of the industry. Yet its long-term loss experience was favorable and its reserve against losses adequate. The company was also highly leveraged in comparison with its competitors. Nonetheless, its degree of leverage had declined sharply in the preceding year. Its net income, moreover, was in an upward trend. In addition. Standard & Poor's deemed the company well run and amply diversified. Thus it rated its notes single-A.

As you can see, rating the debt of finance companies is often unusually complex because so many of them are engaged in widely varying businesses. For this reason, in assessing the debt of such companies, judgement is at least as important as statistical ratios.

How Insurance Bonds Are Rated 10

There are some 2300 fire and casualty insurance companies in this country and another 1800 life insurance companies. Both groups have long been very active in the private placement market and have bought millions upon millions worth of bonds issued by other companies. Yet they themselves have rarely issued debt in either the public or the private placement market. As of a recent date, in fact, only about 25 such companies had debt outstanding that was rated by Standard & Poor's. A large part of this was public debt.

The overwhelming majority of such firms are holding companies. They own one or more insurance firms, plus, in some cases, other subsidiaries in fields like consumer financing, leasing, and real estate. They are heavily dependent on the dividends returned to them by these subsidiaries, particularly any insurance subsidiaries. These dividends represent their major source of income.

One reason that insurers have rarely borrowed money in the long-term debt market is that the group as a whole has usually been cash-rich. But this situation may now be changing. In both 1974 and 1975 many fire and casualty companies suffered very sizable underwriting losses, and in the first of these years at least, many also suffered sharp drops in the values of their stock and bond portfolios.

Largely as a result, a sizable number must increase their capital.

Indeed, early in 1975 William W. Amos, a vice president of The First Boston Corp., an investment banking firm, predicted that in the coming decade the fire and casualty companies alone would need to sell $5 billion worth of bonds.

In many ways the job of rating bonds and notes issued by life companies and those issued by fire and casualty companies is similar. Thus Standard & Poor's looks at the same factors—assets, liabilities, investment portfolios, and so forth—in both cases.

Nonetheless, there are important differences involved in rating the debt of the two different kinds of insurers. In general it is more difficult to rate that issued by fire and casualty companies.

One reason is that there are limits on the losses that can be suffered by life companies. Those limits consist of the number of claims likely to be filed with them in a given year and the face amounts of the policies that they have written. As you know, because of mortality tables built up over the years, a life company has a very good idea of how many of its policyholders will die this year, next year, and in the years thereafter.

Fire and casualty companies, by contrast, never know how many catastrophes will take place in a 12-month period, nor do they know the size of the claims that will be filed by their policyholders. And in fact, in both numbers and amounts, claims have historically proved highly cyclical. It follows, of course, that both the losses and the earnings of these companies often vary sharply from year to year.

Another reason why it is easier to rate the debt of life companies is that the kinds of investments they may make are closely and conservatively regulated by state insurance commissions. Fire and casualty companies, by contrast, are freer to invest in common stocks, which may markedly affect their capital position, for either better or worse.

All this means, of course, that Standard & Poor's looks at the investment portfolios of fire and casualty companies much more closely than it does those of life companies. It also means that it is virtually impossible for the bonds of a fire and casualty company to receive a triple-A rating. At least no such bonds presently carry that rating. The earnings—and, therefore, the fixed-charge coverages of such companies—are just too unpredictable.

Most of the information that Standard & Poor's requires of insurance companies is contained in their so-called convention statements. These statements are, in effect, annual reports that each insurer must file with its state insurance commission. They include not only a balance sheet, a

How Insurance Bonds Are Rated

summary of operations, an analysis of reserves against losses, and so forth, but also a detailed listing of investment holdings and trades. Such statements may run 100 or more pages in length, and Standard & Poor's wants to see them for each of the past 5 years.

Naturally, it wants other information, too. Much of this can be garnered in conversations with management.

As always, the investment advisory organization first looks at the indenture of an insurance company bond. It demands, or at least prefers, many of the same clauses that it demands or prefers in the indentures of other kinds of bonds. Thus it wants the company to promise not to issue any debt senior to the debt in question. It may also want the company to agree that its net assets must exceed its debt by a certain margin before it can issue new debt, and it may want the firm to establish a sinking fund so that much of the debt can be retired before it matures.

Often Standard & Poor's wants an insurance holding company to include another clause. Assuming that the company has three or four insurance firms among its subsidiaries, the investment advisory organization may want it to promise not to sell the major subsidiary.

There are at least two reasons for this. One, the major subsidiary is likely to provide most of the funds needed to pay off the debt's principal and interest. Two, Standard & Poor's likes a company to stick to its basic business—insurance. As we will learn more fully later on, it believes that some insurance companies regard themselves less as insurers than as vehicles for making investments in stocks and bonds.

Standard & Poor's next looks at a company's size and at its competitive position within its industry. As James J. O'Meara, an analyst, puts it: "A company of good size and high rank is apt to get the best business. It can also better withstand a major loss or mistake. A small or medium-sized company may be ruined by plunging into a new kind of insurance that hasn't been properly priced."

Next, the insurer's assets come under scrutiny. These assets usually include bonds, mortgages, and stocks. Although Standard & Poor's emphasis is on the investment portfolio as a whole, it carefully examines each part of it.

In the case of bonds it is interested in their quality, marketability, and maturity, as well as with the value at which the insurer carries them on its books and with the proportion that are tax-exempt.

It tries to ascertain whether the insurer is obtaining a reasonable rate of return in comparison with what it has obtained in the past and with what other insurers obtain. It also tries to determine whether the insurer is speculating by investing in too many bonds with relatively low ratings.

So far as marketability goes, the investment advisory organization mainly wants to be sure that the insurer has not invested in private placements to an excessive degree. Such bonds are less marketable than others.

Standard & Poor's also checks whether a reasonable number of the bonds mature each year. This helps provide the insurer with ready cash, for whatever purpose.

The tax laws allow insurance companies to disregard (not report) one-half of the income they earn from underwriting life insurance policies, provided this income is retained for the benefit of their policyholders. As a result, life companies have less need for tax-exempt income than many other kinds of firms. Thus if they have a lot of tax-exempt bonds in their portfolios, Standard & Poor's wants to know why. They could ordinarily earn more from corporate bonds.

The insurer's mortgage holdings are also looked into. Commercial mortgages in particular can be very risky. Accordingly, Standard & Poor's carefully checks the number and kind of defaults the insurer may have suffered.

It also looks into any conventional mortgages and any mortgages insured by either the Federal Housing Administration or the Veterans Administration that the insurer may hold. The latter mortgages are considered superior to the first kind. Yet provided the conventional mortgages an insurer holds seem sound and provided its other investments seem reasonably liquid, Standard & Poor's is not apt to be unduly concerned about the proportion of conventional mortgages the insurer owns.

From mortgages, Standard & Poor's turns its attention to stocks and is particularly interested in what proportion of the insurer's total assets they represent. If it is studying a life company and if stocks represent more than 10 percent of the company's portfolio, the investment advisory organization may be concerned. After all, the prices of stocks can fluctuate greatly.

The proportion of preferred stocks to common stocks is also checked. Standard & Poor's likes to see a reasonable balance between the two.

In addition, the tax liability of the insurer is taken into consideration. Some insurers bought stocks so many years ago that the convention-

How Insurance Bonds Are Rated

statement worth of their holdings must be partly discounted because of the heavy capital gains taxes that would have to be paid if the stocks were sold.

In the case of life companies, Standard & Poor's also looks with unusual care at the total value of the loans they have made to their policyholders. As you know, policyholders have a right to borrow from their insurers, and the insurers have no control over the exercise of this right.* "But," says James O'Meara, "every time an insurer lends a dollar to a policyholder, it has one less dollar to invest in bonds, mortgages, and stocks, which currently yield more than the 5 or 6 percent returned by policy loans."

Typically, a stock life company's policy loans amount to less than 10 percent of its total assets, a mutual life company's to less than 15 percent. If these loans rise as high as 15 and 20 percent respectively, it is cause for concern, particularly if the loans remain at this level for several years. In all probability such a development would weigh against the insurer in the rating process.

As you can guess, the investment advisory organization also looks into the total yield from the insurer's assets. What counts is how this yield stacks up against the insurer's past record and the current records of its competitors. In 1974 life companies enjoyed an average annual yield of 6.25 percent. As always, fire and casualty companies' average yield was considerably lower because they invest so heavily in common stocks.

Finally, Standard & Poor's wants to know whether an insurer has any so-called nonadmitted assets and, if so, what proportion of its total assets these represent. State insurance commissions are apt to be conservative and may not allow an insurer to count some of its assets as assets.

For example, they may disallow any foreign reinsurance a company holds on the grounds that a foreign insurer may not pay off. Again, if a portfolio includes only triple-B bonds, they may disallow some of the value of these bonds. They prefer better balanced portfolios that contain some bonds rate A and better.

The point is, Standard & Poor's feels compelled to look at an insurer's assets in the same way state insurance commissions do. If an unusual

---

*Policies issued by fire and casualty companies do not accumulate a cash value and cannot be borrowed against.

proportion of the assets have been declared nonadmitted, it takes this factor into consideration in making its rating.

Standard & Poor's next turns to an insurer's liabilities. Depending on the nature of the company, it looks at its reserves, its claims in process, its mandatory security valuation reserve, and its capitalization.

There are many approved ways of establishing reserves. But Standard & Poor's prefers to see them established very conservatively. In the case of a life company, a key question is what rate of interest it assumes it will earn on that portion of its premiums that it invests. The lower its assumption, the more safely it is operating, because it is putting aside more dollars in its reserves than it otherwise would. In the case of a casualty company, the assumed rate of interest is much less important because its reserves are of such a short-term nature.

Questions about claims in process primarily relate to casualty companies. This is because claims are often contested, and the ultimate amount of payments the companies must make is difficult to predict.

How does a company's actual claims experience compare with what the company thought it would be as of 5 years ago? In establishing reserves against claims, has the company historically made sufficient allowance for inflation? Is it settling enough claims out of court? If not, it runs a risk that juries will award more to claimants than they would receive in settlements.

Questions about the mandatory security valuation reserve are made only in reference to life companies. These companies establish such a reserve against possible sharp fluctuations in the value of their equity. Drops in the amount of the reserve may be cause of concern.

When it turns to capitalization, Standard & Poor's is interested in how much premium volume an insurer writes in relation to its capital. In the case of a casualty company in particular, it does not like the ratio to exceed three to one. If the ratio runs higher, the company may be exposing itself unduly to heavy claims and losses further down the road.

The investment advisory organization is also interested in the debt and equity position of the parent company and in how it intends to use the proceeds obtained from the sale of debt. Investment of the proceeds in speculative ventures invariably necessitates a tightening of the normal parameters used in the rating process.

Naturally, Standard & Poor's takes cognizance of the kinds of insurance an insurer sells. It is particularly interested in the mix of a company's policies and is certain to compare this mix with those of other companies. In the case of life companies, whole life insurance tends to be the safest and most profitable. Term insurance is the next safest and most profitable, group insurance considerably less so. Accident and health policies often serve as loss leaders.

The investment advisory organization also checks whether the company sells participating (dividend-paying) or nonparticipating policies. If the former, management determines how much it pays out to its policyholders; what is left over goes into stockholders' surplus. If the company pays too much to its policyholders, it may not build up a sufficient surplus. The criterion, of course, is how it stacks up against the industry.

Does the insurer sell gimmick policies—e.g., special policies geared solely to, say, people suffering from cancer or to students or to retired people? Although some such policies can be highly profitable, many are largely untested over a period of time.

Not unnaturally, Standard & Poor's checks the lapse ratio of life companies. An increase in the number of people who let their policies lapse may indicate that a company's salesmen are selling too aggressively to people who cannot afford to pay premiums. This can be expensive. A company may even show a loss when such policies are terminated.

In the case of fire and casualty companies, Standard & Poor's is primarily interested in what proportion of their policies involve insurance in which claims and settlements may not be made until years after the events on which the claims are based. Malpractice insurance sold to physicians, hospitals, and others is the major case in point. Because of inflation and ever-increasing jury awards, it is difficult to provide reserves against such claims with any assurance that they will be sufficient. As a result, Standard & Poor's likes to see as little such insurance as possible.

Over how wide an area does a fire and casualty company sell its insurance? The wider, the better. The dispersion of risk lessens the impact of a catastrophe.

Marketing practices are also examined. The investment advisory organization wants to know whether the insurer has its own agency force, uses independent brokers, or employs mail or other mass-marketing techniques. The method used gives some indication of the quality of a firm.

If it has its own agents, the insurer has complete control over them. Yet how well does it police them? And to what extent does the force suffer from turnover?

If the insurer uses brokers, it has less control. Then the question is, How well does it service the brokers? If it does not do well by them, they will give most of their quality business to other companies.

What type of policyholder does the insurer seek? Some life companies sell heavily to executives, who, of course, are apt to buy the biggest and most profitable policies. Yet they are also apt to exercise their right to borrow against the policies. Thus Standard & Poor's examines such an insurer's policy loans ratio with care. Other life companies sell heavily to blue collar workers. These workers are less apt to be aware of their right to borrow, but more apt to buy smaller policies. In this case the insurer's lapse ratio may be of greater importance.

The amount of reinsurance an insurer carries on its policies is also checked. In general Standard & Poor's prefers that a life insurer retain—that is not, reinsure—as much of its business as possible. When it does not reinsure too much, it is one sign that the company is stable and confident. In the case of a fire and casualty company, Standard & Poor's likes the insurer to carry sufficient catastrophe coverage to limit the impact of unusually large losses.

To the extent that a company does reinsure, the investment advisory organization wants to know how much reinsurance it carries, at what policy level the reinsurance takes effect, and with whom the reinsurance is placed. It may be concerned if the company relies too heavily on one reinsurer or if it places a great deal with little-known foreign reinsurers. State insurance commissioners may not give credence to certain foreign reinsurers.

As it does with all companies, Standard & Poor's studies the quality and quantity of an insurer's sources of income. Obviously, these sources include underwriting and investments.

The key question about underwriting profits is how they compare with those of other members of the industry. If they vary sharply from year to year—or, in the case of casualty companies, vary more than would seem normal—Standard & Poor's looks closely at the size of the swings.

The traditional measure of underwriting performance for the fire and casualty insurance industry is the so-called combined ratio,* which reflects a company's expenses and losses as opposed to its revenues.

---

*The combined ratio is the sum of the loss ratio (losses and loss adjustment expense as a percentage of earned premiums) and the expense ratio (underwriting expenses as a percentage of premiums written).

When expenses and losses are less than revenues, a profit is usually indicated.

Says O'Meara: "It is comforting when a company's combined ratio is fairly consistent, as this tends to indicate the company is reserving enough money in good years to meet the claims that will arise in bad years."

Standard & Poor's also compares an insurer's investment profits with those of the industry. It is also concerned with how these profits compare with the firm's own underwriting profits.

Says O'Meara: "Some casualty companies seem to take planned losses in underwriting in order to obtain money to invest. They seem to regard themselves primarily as investors rather than as insurers. These companies are not worth as much as those with sustained underwriting profits. They also represent greater risks. As everyone knows, there's always the possibility that underwriting will get out of control and that investment income will not be sufficient to produce an overall profit."

Naturally, in studying an insurer's underwriting and investment income, Standard & Poor's examines its fixed-charge coverage. In reality it is usually looking at the ability of the insurance subsidiaries to return enough in dividends to cover the principal and interest on the holding company's debt.

In the case of life insurance holding companies, Standard & Poor's likes earnings to cover interest at least three times over. Coverage of this order makes a company a candidate for a rating of at least triple-B. Because of possible volatility in earnings, the coverage of a casualty company should be, on average, even higher.

Nonetheless, these are not hard-and-fast rules. If a holding company owns debt-intensive subsidiaries, like finance or real estate firms, its coverage can differ dramatically from the desirable norm.

When it turns to management, Standard & Poor's is particularly concerned with the background of the men running the company. Observes O'Meara: "Marketing men are often in charge of life companies. And they can sometimes be overly optimistic."

Whoever is in charge, who backs them up? The firm's actuaries should have shown a great deal of accuracy in their projections. Experienced investment executives are also a must.

Where is the company going? Is it planning to diversify? Although diversification may make a great deal of sense, it entails heavy risks, particularly if the firm is a specialty company.

Does the company have the personnel necessary to diversify? The financing? The controls? Notes O'Meara: "What may look like an attractive expansion to stockholders may scare us. We may think that the company is getting in way over its head."

One other question should interest you: In studying an insurance holding company, to what extent does Standard & Poor's probe the company's subsidiaries? As you have probably inferred, it studies the main insurance subsidiaries very closely. It pays considerably less attention to noninsurance subsidiaries unless they represent a very healthy slice of the business.

The overriding question about insurance subsidiaries is to what extent they are independent. For example, are a great many of the holding company's directors also directors of the subsidiaries? How strict are the regulatory limits on the amount of dividends the holding company may take out of its insurance subsidiaries? Standard & Poor's looks askance at any signs that the holding company can bleed its subsidiaries dry. It likes the subsidiaries to be as independent as possible.

As we have seen, in making any kind of rating, Standard & Poor's usually spends a fair amount of time comparing the issuer with its competitors. Such comparisons are particularly important in the case of insurance companies. "Indeed," says O'Meara, "the real key to rating an insurance firm is to determine how, where, and why it differs from the rest of the industry."

For example, NLT Corp. is a holding company that derived some 96 percent of its 1974 earnings from National Life & Accident Insurance Company, the rest from various other subsidiaries and its investment portfolio. In May 1975 the holding company issued $50 million of 10-year notes, the proceeds from which were advanced to its real estate subsidiary. The subsidiary planned to use them to make short-term mortgage loans.

As Standard & Poor's saw it, NLT suffered from some disadvantages. For one, only recently had National Life's yield on investments begun to approach the industry norm. For another, the lapse ratio on its policies was higher than average.

On the other hand, National Life then ranked among the nation's top half-dozen stockholder-owned insurance companies in terms of assets. Furthermore, the issue represented NTL's only long-term debt and amounted to only 5.6 percent of its 1974 capitalization. Also, NTL's net tangible assets totaled more than 1000 percent of this debt. Deeming the firm's financial strength "overwhelming," Standard & Poor's rated the issue triple-A.

How Foreign Bonds Are Rated   11

Years ago many foreign governments and corporations sold bonds in this country's long-term debt market. Then in 1963 the United States Government imposed a so-called interest equalization tax on any investments made in foreign securities. The tax amounted to 11.25 percent and was designed to curb an outflow of dollars to countries overseas. It proved so effective that issuance of foreign securities all but ceased on these shores. Early in 1974, however, the United States Government reduced the tax to zero. Although there has not been quite the rush to market that some experts had forecast, an increasing number of foreign governments and corporations have sold their securities to American investors in the ensuing two-plus years. The European Coal & Steel Community, for example, sold $100 million of bonds in late 1974, then another $150 million in early 1975, and yet another $150 million in late 1975.

There are plenty of reasons why foreign organizations sometimes hesitate to borrow here. Among other things, they often have to adjust their financial statements to meet the accounting requirements of the Securities & Exchange Commission.

On the other hand, there are also reasons why they like to borrow here. The principal one is that they can usually borrow larger amounts of money for longer periods of time and occasionally at lower rates of

99

interest than they can obtain in, say, the European market (Euromarket).

In any case, in September 1974 Standard & Poor's began rating debt securities issued in the United States by both foreign corporations and governments. It had already been rating Canadian issues for some time.

The investment advisory organization requires the following information from foreign corporations: a demonstrated operating record and audited financial statements for at least the last 5 years; a complete outline of the terms of the issue, the proposed use of the proceeds, and detailed copies of the company's most recent interim balance sheet and income statement; income statements; balance sheets, and source and application of fund forecasts for several years into the future; an outline of the company's basic business, most important objectives, markets, and competition; possibly a face-to-face meeting with management to discuss past performance, future plans, and related matters; and any other information that will be helpful to an understanding and evaluation of the issue. In this connection, if there is any link between an issuing corporation and a government—whether it involves a guarantee, subsidy, ownership, regulation of operations, or some other matter—Standard & Poor's wants to know what it is.

On top of this, Standard & Poor's requires foreign corporate issuers to meet four special criteria: First, they must inform the investment advisory organization of the major differences between their accounting principles and those commonly used in this country. Second, they must retain a paying agent in this country to handle interest payments and other debt requirements. Third, they must specify in their issuing documents that they will allow themselves to be sued in an American court by any bondholders seeking to enforce the provisions of their contracts. Finally, they must provide specific assurance that they will be able to make payments of interest and principal in United States dollars, regardless of any problems they may face in international currency.

In rating foreign corporate bonds, Standard & Poor's studies the same five areas that it studies in the case of most American corporate bonds: indenture or issuing documents, asset protection, financial resources, future earning power, and management.

Thus, in the case of the indenture, the investment advisory organization is certain to ask: Does it prohibit the issuer from selling additional bonds that would be equal or senior to those presently being issued?

How Foreign Bonds Are Rated

Does it impose a restriction on the total amount of debt that can be outstanding or that may be issued? Does it require establishment of a sinking fund into which the issuer must make annual contributions toward repayment of principal? Is there any mortgage or lien on the issuer's revenues? Does the issuer have a reserve fund that it can turn to in an emergency?

In studying asset protection, Standard & Poor's checks the makeup of the issuer's working capital, including the quality of its receivables and inventories; the character of its land, buildings, equipment, and other properties and the extent to which these properties have been added to or improved on in the last 5 years; its accounting practices; the saleability of its securities, and the difference, if any, between their book and market values.

In addition, Standard & Poor's checks four ratios that tell a great deal about the company's asset protection. These ratios are working capital to debt; debt to net property; debt to net property, plus investments; and net tangible assets as a percentage of debt.

Financial resources are always important to a corporate issuer, domestic or foreign. Thus Standard & Poor's carefully checks the amount of the issuer's cash and working capital. They are good indicators of its ability to operate in any kind of economic climate and still make interest and sinking fund payments. They also provide some indication of whether it will need to borrow more in the future.

Among the questions that the investment advisory organization asks are, Has there been a recent downturn in the company's cash position? How much cash is internally generated in relation to capital expenditures? How extensive is the company's use of short-term debt and for what purpose is it used? Has the company historically been too dependent on banks? Is its dividend policy too liberal in comparison with those of its competitors? Thus not just the size but also the character of the company's resources plays a role in Standard & Poor's assessment.

Future earnings protection is the fourth major area Standard & Poor's looks at. As we saw in the case of domestic corporate bonds, it wants to know what industry the company is in—in particular whether it is a growth industry or a mature one. It is also interested in the company's position in that industry and in its individual record. Thus, even though the company may not be an industry leader, it may have increased its sales and earnings or made other recent advances.

Does the company have good financial controls? Does it set aside enough toward depreciation? Does it pay out too much in dividends? And are its tax practices sufficiently conservative? On most of these matters, Standard & Poor's tries to compare the company with its competitors.

The investment advisory organization also studies the company's fixed-charge coverage—that is, the number of times its earnings exceed the interest it must pay. It looks at the past, present and likely future of this coverage and is particularly interested in the trend of coverage, including coverage of rental fees, after taxes. Ordinarily a company's debt cannot hope to qualify for a rating of triple-B—the minimum that most companies in this country hope to achieve—unless coverage is at least two times interest and rental payments.

Finally, Standard & Poor's turns to management. As always, the investment advisory organization is interested in its policies and objectives, its research and development projects, its new product plans, its cash flow projections, its acquisition philosophy, and in anything else that will shed light on the company's probable future.

In rating domestic corporate bonds, Standard & Poor's ordinarily considers future earning power and management more important than the first three factors put together. This sometimes does and sometimes does not prove true in its rating of foreign corporate bonds. According to Brenton W. Harries, president of Standard & Poor's: "The weight each of the five factors receives varies, depending on the nature of a company's business."

There are other important differences between the rating of domestic and foreign corporate bonds. For one thing, although Standard & Poor's applies the same standards and ratios to both kinds of bonds, it does not necessarily expect to come up with the same figures. Roy Weinberger, a manager in Standard & Poor's corporate finance department, cites one example that helps explain why:

In Japan, the sources of capital funds are much fewer than here. As a result, Japanese companies borrow significantly more from banks than American firms do. This is accepted business practice and is fully supported by government policy. Therefore, a level of bank borrowings that would be regarded as dangerously high for an American company can be considered acceptable in the context of the Japanese system.

Because of this phenomenon, we obtain different results when we calculate such ratios as fixed-charge coverage and debt to capitalization. We find a lower ratio in the first instance and higher ratio in the second than we would find in the case of an American company of the same general caliber.

For another thing, says Weinberger, a foreign company must be judged in terms of its position in its own markets, not America's. "Thus," he explains, "a leading French chemical company may be only one-fifth as big as an American chemical company. But this does not necessarily mean that the French company is a poorer credit risk."

For a third thing, Standard & Poor's must pay attention to the political context in which a company operates. The basic questions are; How stable is the government in question, and how willing is it to foster growth in its economy?

The answers may involve possible bankruptcy on the part of foreign governments, with all the dire consequences that would result. The threat is not an idle one. In recent years both England and Italy have teetered near the edge of the precipice.

There is also a danger that some foreign countries may be taken over by Communist or other kinds of totalitarian governments. In such cases the new governments may not permit corporations within their boundaries to honor their commitments to their creditors. Indeed, the new governments may not even honor the commitments of the governments that preceded them.

This is exactly what has happened in the case of several Eastern European countries. Before World War II, these countries issued long-term bonds in the American market. Then, after the war, Communist governments took over, and the bonds were defaulted upon. Very recently, there has been some restitution—but only years after the bonds had matured. Furthermore, the restitution was far from complete. Poland, for example, agreed to pay a mere 40 percent of the face value of its bonds in full settlement of all claims.

As an example of how Standard & Poor's rates foreign debt, let us look at a recent issue from ICI North America, a wholly owned subsidiary of Imperial Chemical Industries Limited. The parent company is headquartered in England and owns more than 400 subsidiaries and associated companies in 55 countries. In June 1975 ICI North America issued $100 million of 20-year sinking fund debentures in the United States market. The debentures were guaranteed by the parent company.

Standard & Poor's found that the sales and net income of the group as a whole had begun to slip in the early months of 1975 and believed that income would be down for the full year. On the other hand, sales had risen 36 percent in the preceding year and income 31 percent. Furthermore, the group's after-tax fixed-charge coverage amounted to nearly three and seven-tenths times interest and rental payments. Its net tangible assets totaled nearly three times long-term debt, its working capital more than 57 percent of debt. Said Standard & Poor's:

> ICI has demonstrated its strength in terms of sales and earnings consistently in recent years under difficult circumstances. Besides good product diversification, the group has broad geographical diversification both in and outside of Europe. Also, conservative management practices with respect to the group's finances have resulted in a sound financial position. Based on these factors, we have rated the issue double-A.

Before looking at how Standard & Poor's rates the debt issues of foreign governments, it is worth noting that late in 1975 the investment advisory organization began rating Eurobonds. These are bonds sold in the European market by American corporations or by foreign corporations or governments. Because they are sold outside this country, they are not registered with the SEC. As this is written, Standard & Poor's has assessed only two such bonds. Both were sold by French petroleum firms, and both were given ratings of double-A.

Suffice it to say that Standard & Poor's requires the same kind and amount of information on Eurobonds as it does on foreign bonds sold in the American market. It also assesses Eurobonds in the same fashion.

Yet there are a few differences. One of the most important is that although the investment advisory organization assesses the terms of the indentures under which the bonds are issued, it makes no attempt to assess the ability of Eurobondholders to enforce indenture covenants. Another, as noted earlier, is that the rating agency demands a clear explanation of the accounting principles used and, when these principles differ substantially from United States practice, a statement of the historical or other basis of their use.

Let us now turn to issues of foreign governments or their agencies, either of which may sell bonds in the United States or other overseas markets. Standard & Poor's began rating such issues in 1975 and, near the end of that year, had rated five, including bonds issued or guaranteed by the governments of Austria, Australia, France, Norway, and Japan. All five were given ratings of triple-A. One other foreign government sought a rating, but when it learned that its issue would be rated single-A, it withdrew its request. National governments, it would seem, have difficult in accepting less than the highest possible rating.

How Foreign Bonds Are Rated

The basic minimum information that Standard & Poor's requires from a foreign government, government agency, or corporation whose debt carries some kind of government guarantee or participation includes the following: balance of payments data for the past 5 years, including a discussion of monetary, trade, and other factors that have affected the components of the balance; the most recent statement of the country's international reserves; government debt data, with domestic and foreign debt shown separately, plus a repayment schedule of both principal and interest in the case of foreign direct and guaranteed debt; the most recent data on foreign trade, broken down by commodity group and by trading partners, plus a discussion of any major changes in the statistics in recent years; a yearbook or other text or material that discusses the country's natural resources, principal industries, demography, banking system, governmental structure, legislative system, budget-preparation system, plus the relationship among industry, labor, and government; any recent economic studies done by the nation's central bank, some other recognized authority, or an important outside organization, such as the International Monetary Fund; and, finally, a discussion of the nation's borrowing needs, the purposes for which any monies raised will be used, and the government's attitude toward private investment. It is worth emphasizing that, in the case of government-guaranteed corporate debt, all this information is in addition to that required of the corporation itself.

Obviously, this is a wealth of information, and in many instances more is required. Indeed, Standard & Poor's often wants to meet with the banking, industry, and government leaders of the nation in question. As a result, these pages do not permit a detailed discussion of all the areas that Standard & Poor's probes. But three broad areas can be delineated.

First, it looks into the country's entire political, economic, and social structure. It is interested in anything that bears on this structure and on the government's ability to operate effectively under it. For example, does the government have the ability and power to take needed economic measures even though the measures may be unpopular?

Second, the investment advisory organization looks at the country's overall economy. What are the nation's physical characteristics? How self-sufficient is it in terms of food, fuel, and other basic resources? What can and does it export—and to whom? How sophisticated is its financial structure? What is the relationship between banks and industry and among banks, industry, and government?

Third, Standard & Poor's checks the country's relationship with the international financial community. How extensive are its financial reserves? How much flexibility does it have to deal with ups and downs in its currency and with ups and downs in the international economy? How able is it to market debt outside its shores?

This, then, will give you a rough idea of how Standard & Poor's goes about rating the bonds and notes of foreign governments. Let us see now why it gave a triple-A rating to $100 million of medium-term notes recently issued by Norway. The country planned to use the proceeds from the sale to help it meet an anticipated deficit in its balance of payments.

As Standard & Poor's saw it, since World War II the Norwegian government had striven to encourage economic growth, both in general and on a regionally balanced basis, to transfer productive resources and employment from primary sectors of the economy to industry and services, and to develop capital-intensive industries. Furthermore, its total domestic production of goods and services had increased in every postwar year, its registered number of unemployed was low, and the expected deficit in its balance of payments was a recent phenomenon. Said the investment advisory organization:

Although small in physical size and population, Norway has a highly developed economy characterized by a high standard of living and a stable social and political system. It has been a successful trading nation, as evidenced by its highly competitive export sector. As a result of the orderly exploitation of its North Sea oil reserves, it will soon be in an advantageous position from a balance-of-payments viewpoint. Based upon these factors and the demonstrated ability of the Norwegian government to manage its external debt, we are rating this issue AAA.

Standard & Poor's method of arriving at a rating of domestic debt and its fees for doing so are discussed in Chapter 3. Most of what is said there applies to foreign debt as well. But perhaps a couple of points need amplification.

Standard & Poor's fee for an initial rating of foreign debt generally ranges between $5000 and $20,000. The exact amount depends on the time and effort needed to arrive at a rating. If the issuer comes back to the market 6 or 8 months later, the fee may be only one-third to one-half as much as the original, but if it returns 3 or 4 years later, the fee will undoubtedly fall within the initial range because so much data will again have to be reviewed in depth.

How Foreign Bonds Are Rated

Like certain issuers of domestic debt, foreign governments and corporations do not have their debt rated automatically. They must ask to have it rated. Furthermore, they do not have to accept the ratings given. If they do not the ratings are never published. Nevertheless, the issuers are still liable for payment of the investment advisory organization's fee.

So much for foreign debt. We will probably see more such debt sold on these shores in the years ahead. But how much more will depend on how receptive investors here are to such debt, to relative levels of interest rates here and abroad, and to related matters.

How Commercial Paper Is Rated 12

As you know, commercial paper is an unsecured promissory note issued by a financial, industrial, or other kind of corporation. It is issued for periods ranging from 1 to 270 days and ordinarily comes in minimum units of $100,000. Usually, in fact, a unit is many times that figure.

The issuer sells the paper at a discount from its face value. Thus the difference between what the issuer receives and what he pays back represents the interest or rate of return. It should be noted, however, that much commercial paper is rolled over—that is, is sold continuously rather than being paid off.

By edict of the SEC, the money raised by means of commercial paper must be used as working capital. Thus it cannot be employed to purchase plant and equipment, to finance real estate developments, to purchase securities, or to fulfill other long-range purposes.

Why do companies issue such paper? It is almost always cheaper than borrowing from a bank. The interest rate is usually lower than a bank's prime rate. Even when this is not the case, the compensating balance that a bank requires almost invariably makes paper less costly. To top it all off, commercial paper provides its issuer with an additional source of working capital.

For the buyer, commercial paper also offers advantages. The chief one is that paper usually returns more interest than United States Treasury bills and other short-term investments.

For all these reasons, you might think that the commercial paper market was a big, booming business, and in one sense it is. As recently as 1962 the annual market totaled $6 billion. By 1975 it was running in excess of $50 billion.

Nonetheless, there are only about 730 issuers of commercial paper in this country at the present time. This figure includes several score companies that issue paper only within the regions in which they operate. They are not well enough known to tap the national market.

Most of the remaining 600 or so issuers are big, well-known firms, apt to appear on *Fortune*'s lists of the nation's first or second 500 largest companies. Standard & Poor's rates the paper of more than two-thirds of these 600 or so firms.

As you can deduce, the investment advisory organization rates such paper only on request, and the paper's issuers can reject the ratings if they wish. When a rating is accepted, Standard & Poor's publishes it and the reasons behind it in one or more of its various publications. The rating is also disseminated in circulars put out by the issuer's commercial paper dealer.*

What information does Standard & Poor's require commercial paper issuers to provide? This varies somewhat, depending on whether the issuer is an industrial, financial, or other kind of corporation. In general it requires the same information that it would require if the issuer were about to put out a long-term bond.

Standard & Poor's also requires the issuer to include a letter requesting a rating; a complete list of its bank lines, plus the name of each bank, its commitment, and a contact at the bank; a hand-signed, certified copy of the board of directors' authorization to issue commercial paper; the names and telephone numbers of two persons at the issuing company; the name of the commercial paper dealer that is being used, if applicable; a complete set of the company's financial statements for the past 5 years; an explanation of its reasons for issuing commercial paper; an explanation of its future short-term and long-term financing requirements and of its plans for fulfilling these requirements; an estimate of the amount of paper that will be outstanding in the foreseeable future; and a statement on the current status of its operations.

In addition, Standard & Poor's almost invariably wants to talk with

---

*Some issues of commercial paper are marketed through dealers. Most are marketed directly by their issuers. These latter issuers consist almost exclusively of large finance companies.

How Commercial Paper Is Rated

the issuing company's management unless it has done so in the recent past. In a moment we'll look at the kind of information it seeks in these meetings, although it includes some of the matters cited immediately above.

Finally, the investment advisory organization requires commercial paper issuers to provide it with supplemental information each and every quarter and in some cases oftener. This information includes a quarterly balance sheet, a quarterly income statement, an indication of the amount of paper outstanding at the moment, and an estimate of the amount that will be outstanding in the next quarter, plus immediate notification of any changes in the issuer's bank lines, long-term financing plans, or corporate structure. In the case of any particular company, of course, still more information may be requested.

From all that has been said, it should be obvious that the job of rating commercial paper is the same from industry to industry and that it also varies from industry to industry. It is the same in that the basic nature of what Standard & Poor's is looking for, its procedures and its thinking are alike. It is different in that the precise information Standard & Poor's seeks, the questions it asks, and the statistical ratios it employs vary somewhat.

Adds Juliette L. Gould, who is in charge of rating these issues: "The weight that we give various factors sometimes varies somewhat from company to company. What can be an avoidable or easily surmountable problem for one company can be a real headache for another. For example, one firm may have a great deal of trouble increasing its bank lines, while another has very little."

In an earlier chapter, we saw the criteria that a corporation must ordinarily meet if its paper is to be rated A-1, A-2, or A-3, which are the only ratings acceptable in the marketplace at this time. These criteria include liquidity ratios adequate to meet the company's cash needs, a rating of triple-B, at a very minimum, on its long-term senior debt, access to at least two additional sources of funds, an upward trend in both earnings and cash flow, and superior management.

But let us look further at what Standard & Poor's studies, using an industrial company as our example, although much of what will be said applies to other kinds of companies as well. Obviously, the investment advisory organization pays some attention to the issuer's long-term debt and to the factors it assays in rating such debt.

The bond's indenture is not important because it has little bearing on commercial paper. The asset protection behind the bond is of somewhat greater importance, because a low level of protection may cause the bond to receive a mediocre rating and thus generally impair the firm's ability to raise money.

Of particular significance is the relation between the company's total liabilities and its stockholders' equity. Standard & Poor's is apt to become very concerned if this ratio is greater than one to one, especially if a greater ratio is not typical for the industry the company is in. Exceptions are made in the case of industries that are regularly affected by seasonal factors.

For example, a canning company's liabilities ordinarily soar between the time crops are harvested and the time canned goods are brought to market. As a result, its liabilities to equity ratio may rise substantially before sinking back to a more normal level.

When it turns to a company's financial condition, Standard & Poor's looks at many of the same factors it looks at in assaying bonds: the company's current ratio, its inventory-turnover rate, its collection rate on accounts receivable, and its dividend policies. As in the case of bonds, the rating agency ordinarily prefers that current assets exceed current liabilities by at least two to one, although the ratio that is common throughout a given industry is also taken into account. In other matters, it compares the issuer against its own past record and against the current and past records of comparable corporations.

Naturally, it is also interested in the issuer's relationships with banks. In general it wants the issuer to have unused bank lines equal to whatever sum it plans to raise in the commercial paper market. In this connection the investment advisory organization gives no weight whatsoever to banks' letters of credit. In fact, if the commercial paper is backed primarily by letters of credit, the paper is not even rated. Explains Ms. Gould: "If we tried to rate such commercial paper, we would end up rating the banks, not the paper issuers."

Standard & Poor's also asks: Is the company's proposed short-term debt as a percentage of its current liabilities out of line with what it has been in the past? Is the proposed debt so large that the company will not be able to pay it off out of cash flow in the foreseeable future? Is the company carrying over short-term debt from one year to the next without any real hope of ever paying it off? Is it in a position to issue additional long-term debt or equity?

When it tries to estimate future earning power, Standard & Poor's again asks many of the same questions it asks of a company seeking to issue bonds: What industry is the company in, and what is the likely future of that industry? Is the company a leader in the industry and, therefore, in a good position to weather a recession? Are its depreciation practices in line with those used in its industry? Does it have good internal financial controls?

The investment advisory organization also looks at the company's coverage of its interest and rental charges. As Ms. Gould points out: "If the company's coverage of its debt is weak, then there is only a small degree of protection for either the long-term or short-term debtholder."

As we have seen, for a company's paper to obtain a rating of A-1, A-2, or A-3, both earnings and cash flow must be on an upward trend. In this regard Standard & Poor's studies the relation between the issuer's net income and its sales. Acceptable percentages vary from industry to industry.

In sum, Standard & Poor's goes over every item on the issuer's balance sheet and income statement. It wants to know if these items are out of line in any material fashion with the company's own track record or with the track records of its competitors. If so, it probes further.

Management is also closely assessed, in much the same fashion it would be if it were planning a bond issue. What are its policies, goals, and objectives? What will implementing these objectives cost? What are its cash flow projections? Its acquisition plans? Its new product plans? And so forth.

Ms. Gould adds three important comments:

First, we are very aware that the managements of some companies simply don't change with the times. They are not alert to new opportunities nor to new competitive trends. Sometimes they are slow to make use of new management tools, although many companies appear to have made great strides in this regard in recent years.

Second, we are very inquisitive about companies that diversify into totally new fields, unrelated to their own. We wonder in particular whether management can handle something completely different and whether it will retain the managements of the companies it acquires.

Third, we like companies to be open with us about their near-term prospects and problems. After all, we operate on a confidential basis. And to pick up a newspaper and read that a company has run into a major problem or has made an important acquisition doesn't sit well with us.

Ms. Gould emphasizes that companies that plan to enter the commercial paper market should work closely with their dealers. "A good dealer," she stresses, "acts as a counselor to its clients. It prepares them for the kind of questions we ask. It also serves as an important liaison between them and us. More than once, we have had to ask a dealer to emphasize our concern to a company about this matter or that."

Now let us see how all these criteria were applied to three different companies during 1975.

AMP is a high technology company and a world leader in the production of electrical devices and related equipment. Historically, it has had an innovative management. At the time in question, its liquidity ratios were down somewhat from previous highs, but seemed likely to improve. It also had a relatively small amount of long-term debt outstanding, and this debt was rated double-A.

Said Standard & Poor's in a formal report: "The company has an impressive record of sales growth and almost uninterrupted earnings increases, year to year, over an extended period. Its profit margins are consistently good, its cash flow strong and improving, and its capitalization conservative." As you can guess, its paper was rated A-1.

Dayton Hudson is a diversified owner of department and specialty stores, operating in a highly competitive environment. Its earnings had been on a plateau for several years, but Standard & Poor's felt management had recognized and overcome several of its problems. Also, the company's long-term debt was rated A, and it was in a position to issue more, plus possibly equity. Said Standard & Poor's: "Its conservative use of short-term debt, satisfactory liquidity ratios, and ready access to the long-term debt market merit our rating its commercial paper A-2."

VSI Corporation manufactures metal products used in various industries and is the recognized leader in certain of its product lines. At the time the rating of its paper was reviewed, in August 1975, its net income had fallen by more than 10 percent from the previous year.

On the other hand, its acid test and current ratios had improved markedly from the earlier year. Said Standard & Poor's: "Because of this company's strong position in its various specialized areas of operations, its more than sufficient bank lines, and its relatively conservative capitalization structure, we are maintaining its A-3 rating."

As you can see, rating commercial paper is every bit as complex as rating long-term bonds, and the job is approached in much the same fashion. Indeed, perhaps the major difference between the two is that more emphasis is placed on a commercial paper issuer's liquidity—that is, its ability to pay off or roll over its paper within a few weeks or months.

How Municipal Bonds Are Rated 13

There are thousands of municipal bond issues outstanding in this country. Although some are constantly being retired, others are constantly being issued. Indeed, in 1975 alone an estimated $29 billion in new long-term municipal bonds reached the public market.

As we saw in an earlier chapter, the majority of municipal issues are general obligation bonds, usually backed by the full faith and credit of the state or city that sells them. All the rest are revenue bonds, usually backed only by the income from or taxes on specific projects.

Unlike corporations, the public bodies that issue municipal bonds do not have to register these bonds with the SEC. Therefore, investors have historically known much less about the pros and cons of individual municipal bonds than they have about individual corporate bonds.

In 1975, however, the United States Congress amended the Securities Exchange Act of 1934 and, among other things, required underwriters of municipal bonds to provide much more information than had been required in the past. Standard & Poor's, of course, had always required certain information from municipal bond issuers. Such as? In the case of general obligation bonds, 10 separate pieces of information are needed.

First, the investment advisory organization requires a statement of the issuer's overall debt, broken down both as to when each issue will mature and as to the kind of security behind it, that is, the source of the

115

income that will serve to pay off principal and interest. This statement must also indicate the issuer's overlapping debt, that is, its share of the debt of overlapping tax units of which it may be part, such as counties, cities, and school districts.

Second, the issuer must provide its total assessed valuations of property for each of the last 4 years. These valuations must be broken down in two ways: first as to whether the property is realty (commercial, industrial, and residential lands and buildings) or personalty (equipment, inventories and the like); and second as to how the various kinds of realty property are assessed. This second step is necessary so that assessed valuations may be translated into market valuations and more meaningful comparisons made.

Third, the issuer must supply tax-collection statements for each of the last 4 years. Each statement must indicate the amount of taxes collected in the year in question, the amount collected in the ensuing year, and the amount collected as of a recent date. The statement must also indicate the issuer's tax rate for each of the last 4 years and its area's overall rate, which means the total of the rates levied by overlapping tax units.

Fourth, the issuer must provide a recent estimate of the population of its area.

Fifth, it must supply copies of its two most recent annual reports and of its most recent budget.

Sixth, it must send in a list of its 10 largest taxpayers, plus the valuations placed on their properties. When these taxpayers are corporations, the number of each corporation's employees must be included.

Seventh, Standard & Poor's requires a brief description of the area's economy. This description must deal with the nature and character of its economic development, the level of its building activity, and the market valuations of its homes.

Eighth, when applicable, as in the case of a school district, the issuer must indicate its school enrollment in each of the last 10 years.

Ninth, it must indicate its borrowing plans for a reasonable period —say, 5 years—into the future, plus the borrowing plans of overlapping tax units.

Finally, it must delineate its capital-improvement program for the next 5 years. In the case of a state, this would include its plans to build or improve highways and the like. In the case of a city, it would include its plans to build or improve streets, sewerage systems, and so forth.

How Municipal Bonds Are Rated

Standard & Poor's lumps this and other pertinent data it obtains about the issuer, from census data, business journals, and other sources, into four categories: debt factors, administrative factors, economic factors, and current financial account analysis. The last two factors are considered the most important. But let us look at all four, in order of ascending importance.

The first matter that Standard & Poor's looks at under debt factors is the nature of the security behind the bond in question. The investment advisory organization also checks the bond's indenture or resolution. A key question is: Does any law forbid the issuer from selling additional bonds without first obtaining the approval of the voters? If not, does the state constitution or any ordinance impose a limit on the amount of the debt the issuer may incur? If so, what is this limit? How close to it is the issuer?

The investment advisory organization also compares the issuer's existing and proposed debt against three different measures. One is per capita debt. The second is per capita debt in relation to per capita income. The third is debt in relation to the total market valuations of taxable property.

Per capita debt of $400 or less is considered low. Debt of $900 to $1000 is considered high. And debt in excess of $1000 is considered high enough so as to constitute a negative factor in a bond's rating. There are exceptions, however. They involve communities with very high per capita incomes or very high per capita market valuations on property.

Per capita debt amounting to less than 10 percent of per capita income is considered good. Debt amounting to between 10 and 15 percent of such income is viewed as so-so. And debt in excess of 15 percent of such income is deemed a little high.

So far as the third criterion goes, the debt of the overwhelming majority of bond issuers ranges between 5 and 10 percent of the total market valuations of taxable property. Debt that falls on either side of this range is considered low or high and is weighed accordingly.

The trend in the issuer's debt, as a percentage of its per capita income and the market valuations of its property, is also considered. A two- or threefold increase in the span of a few years would probably be held against the issuer. A decrease would be counted in its favor, assuming other factors remain positive.

The rate of debt retirement is also taken into account. In ordinary times municipal bond issuers usually sell debt that will mature in 15 to

25 years. In very recent years, however, there has been a growing trend to issue debt that will mature in an even shorter period. Underwriters find such debt easier to sell.

Short-term debt can, of course, be too short term. A major reason why New York City ran into serious financial difficulties in 1975 was that it constantly had to roll over its short-term debt.

The point is, Standard & Poor's likes to see a balance in a municipal bond issuer's debt structure so that unduly large amounts of debt do not come due in any one year. Such a balance helps make debt retirement orderly.

The investment advisory organization also looks closely at the insurer's debt service costs—its mandatory payments of principal and interest—in relation to its gross revenues. When these costs do not exceed 10 percent of gross revenues, the issuer is ordinarily deemed in a comfortable position. But when they run to 20 or 25 percent of revenues, it is adjudged to be running, or beginning to run, a risk.

Yet much depends on the issuer. If it is a city, debt service costs amounting to 20 percent or more of gross revenues would be a worry. But if it is a county or special-purpose district, the same may not hold true. Some counties spend money on little else than road-building.

Debt history is also looked into. As you can guess, the major question is whether the issuer has ever defaulted on principal or interest payments. Most have not, but those that have are probed closely, especially if their defaults have occurred in the last two or three decades.

Finally, Standard & Poor's asks: How much more money will the issuer need to borrow over the next 5 years? Obviously, most issuers will need to build new facilities, such as schools, or replace old ones.

Thus the key questions are: How does the amount that must be borrowed compare with the amount of debt already outstanding, and how does the amount outstanding compare with what will be retired? If the first figure in either case is high, there may be cause for concern.

When Standard & Poor's turns to administrative factors, it first asks: What is the form of government involved? In other words, does the government have wide-ranging authority and responsibility or not? Most cities do not. For example, they usually cannot impose sales or income taxes without obtaining approval of their state legislatures or, in some cases, without going directly to the voters. This means, of course, that property taxes will provide all or most of the revenues from which principal and interest payments must be made.

How Municipal Bonds Are Rated   119

Because so few local governments can levy taxes, other than property taxes, on their own, this lack is not necessarily a strike against them. But those that do have the ability usually get a plus.

Next, the investment advisory organization looks at management. It is particularly concerned with how professional management is. Says John K. Pfeiffer, vice president of Standard & Poor's bond division: "We're definitely seeing a better class of managers than we once did. This is because of the rise of professional city managers. These men are trained for their jobs, more knowledgeable, and more alert than their predecessors of an earlier era."

The investment advisory organization likes to inquire about the issuer's capital-improvement program and its other long-range plans. In fact, it likes to see these plans, ascertain who prepared them, and study them for evidence of careful thought or haphazardness.

Another tip-off to the quality or lack of quality of management is that many states and cities have incurred heavy pension liabilities for the future. Yet these same states and cities have not always funded these liabilities adequately. Thus a recent study of 44 cities in the state of Pennsylvania shows that they have unfunded pension liabilities in excess of $1 billion. In some communities in other areas of the country, unfunded pension liabilities exceed bonded debt.

This problem is of increasing concern to Standard & Poor's. When municipal management indicates it is aware of and trying to do something about the problem, it usually receives a plus. When it brushes the problem aside, it is apt to receive a minus.

Another administrative factor that Standard & Poor's looks at is any limitations on tax rates. Thus an issuer may be legally barred from levying taxes above a certain rate, or it may be forbidden to set aside more than a certain portion of its taxes to pay off principal and interest on debt. Depending somewhat on how stringent such limitations are, they can be a drawback to the issuer's ability to obtain a high rating.

The issuer's tax-collection experience is also important. One reason for New York City's recent troubles is that it based its revenue projections—and hence its budget—on the assumption that it would collect 100 percent of the taxes owed it in the year owed. As of a recent date, its actual tax-collection rate was around 90 percent.

Standard & Poor's believes that a governmental body that collects 98 percent of the taxes owed in the year that they are owed is doing very well. Even an issuer that collects 95 percent is deemed to be doing reasonably well. A lower rate of collection may be cause for concern, although there are exceptions.

For instance, an issuer may have had a long history of collecting 90 or 91 percent of the taxes owed it in the year owed, then another 7 or 8 percent in the ensuing year. This could be the pattern for a community in an agricultural region.

Finally, the investment advisory organization looks at the issuer's revenue structure and the elasticity of that structure. Thus the issuer may be heavily dependent on a certain kind of tax—say, an income tax. In such case a recession could wreak havoc with both its revenues and its budget.

More and more, Standard & Poor's likes to see a reasonable balance in the kind of taxes levied by a municipal bond issuer. It's the old principle of diversification.

Economic factors play a very important role in Standard & Poor's assessment of municipal bonds. Obviously, the state of an issuer's economy has a direct impact on its ability to service its debt. Says Hyman C. Grossman, a vice president in the municipal bond department: "First and foremost, we look for economic stability. If the tax base is not diverse, then we very much hope that employment opportunities are.

"In this connection we check the stability of employment and how this stability or lack thereof compares with that of nearby areas or comparable states or cities elsewhere. Obviously, the rate of unemployment is also taken into account."

Population is also checked, especially its rate of increase or decline. The normal—and ideal—trend is a gradual increase. Says John Pfeiffer: "A rapid increase in population may be a sign of approaching problems in the form of heightened demand for more hospitals, schools, and other municipal services. A decline, of course, often indicates that problems have already arisen in the form of fewer jobs or a dwindling middle class."

In assessing an issuer's economy, Standard & Poor's also looks into the per capita estimated market values of all taxable properties, the per capita estimated market values of homes, and the per capita volume of wholesale and retail sales. Indeed, the overall economic performance of the issuer, as it stacks up against its particular area, its state, and the nation as a whole, is as important as anything in this category.

Finally, the investment advisory organization makes an analysis of the issuer's current account, in particular its fiscal performance in relation to its budget and its balance sheet. Obviously, the major question is whether the main operating account ended the most recent fiscal year with a surplus, in balance, or with a deficit.

Almost any issuer can end up with a deficit, especially during a recession. "But," says Hyman Grossman, "a closing deficit for three successive years is a decidedly negative factor. We know such a trend cannot be allowed to continue for any length of time."

Yet Standard & Poor's looks well beyond the question of whether the budget is in balance. For example, it wants to know how rapidly the budget is increasing in size.

Avers Richard E. Huff, another vice president in the municipal bond department: "In these inflationary times an increase of only 10 percent a year is considered reasonable, other things being equal. An increase of 20 or 25 percent, however, is considered very worrisome, especially if the tax base is expanding at a much slower rate."

Standard & Poor's also looks into the issuer's current assets. It is particularly interested in its quick assets, i.e., cash and securities that can be quickly marketed. It is somewhat less interested in the amount of federal and state aid the issuer may expect because such aid often arrives late.

In certain instances, however, such aid can be important. For example, some school districts in the state of New York are heavily dependent on state aid. Then the question arises: What happens if the state cannot maintain its present level of giving?

Another matter Standard & Poor's considers is whether an issuer's financial accounts are independently audited. New York City, among others, has long failed to submit to such audits. And this has weighed against it.

Says Richard Huff: "I'd estimate that a majority of states and cities do have their accounts independently audited, but perhaps only a bare majority of the states. What's more, the quality of the audits varies greatly, especially at the state level. We've had instances in which we've received audits two or three years late. By the time we got them, they were of little use."

Finally, Standard & Poor's tries to ascertain whether the issuer engages in any kind of financial gimmickery. This can count heavily against it. New York City, for example, long engaged in gimmickery of various sorts. Thus it got in the habit of using the proceeds from short-term debt to finance long-term capital expenditures and of using the proceeds from long-term debt to pay day-to-day operating expenses, thus violating some very basic rules of financial prudence.

Yet New York has not been the only offender in this regard. Late in 1975 Standard & Poor's lowered its rating on Philadelphia's debt because of that city's operating deficit and its accounting practices. Among other things, it was borrowing from its capital fund to meet its operating budget and counting on revenues that might never materialize.

Debt, administration, economy, and current account factors are, then, the four major areas that Standard & Poor's looks at in weighing general obligation bonds. In light of these factors, let us see how it recently rated two specific issues.

In June 1975 the state of Utah issued $70 million worth of bonds. They are backed by the full faith and credit of the state and are designed to mature serially between 1980 and 1988. About one-half of the proceeds are being used to expand a medical center complex at the University of Utah, the other one-half for other state-financed construction.

As Standard & Poor's saw it, Utah had a couple of strikes against it. First, it is sparsely populated. Second, its per capita income is below the national average.

Yet just about everything else was in its favor. Its trip to the bond market was only its third in 50 years. All of its debt already outstanding will be retired by 1980, before the new issue begins to come due. Its revenues exceeded its expenditures by many millions in both fiscal 1973 and 1974, and the principal and interest payments on its debt accounted for a mere 1 percent of these expenditures. In fact, the state was well enough off so that it had given its citizens a tax rebate in the preceding year. Finally, all its financial operations seemed satisfactory. As a result, Standford & Poor's rated the state's bonds triple-A.

In October 1975 Grand Prairie, Texas issued $4 million worth of general obligation bonds, due to mature serially between 1977 and 1993. The bonds are secured by limited ad valorem taxes, and the proceeds from the sale are being used to build a new fire station, construct and improve streets and drainage systems, and acquire and improve park sites.

In Standard & Poor's view, Grand Prairie had a great deal going for it. It is situated between Dallas and Fort Worth, 20 minutes from the downtown sections of each. It had just been designated an All-American city by the National Municipal League. It had a strong, diversified, and growing economic base, with a number of nationally known companies

How Municipal Bonds Are Rated

in its midst. Its unemployment rate was very low, and its tax-collection rate was excellent.

On the other hand, it had had to use $600,000 in federal revenue sharing funds to maintain its operating budget. Although this budget had made a good recovery in 1975, it had been in deficit in both of the preceding years. Much more important, with the sale of the new issue, the principal and interest payments on the city's debt would amount to better than 19 percent of its expenditures in fiscal 1976. The upshot? Grand Prairie's bonds were rated only A+.

Now let us turn to revenue bonds. Regardless of the precise purpose of a given issue, all issuers of such bonds must supply information in six basic areas.

First, there must be a statement describing the purpose of the issue. This statement must include a breakdown of estimated construction costs, the indicated starting date of the construction, and the expected completion date.

Second, the issuer must provide an engineering report, a feasibility study, or both. This must include a complete history of the system involved, presuming it is already in existence; a statement justifying the need for initial or further construction, with a description of the benefits likely to result; and a list of competitive systems in the area, with an indication of how their services compare with those of the system being proposed.

Third, the issuer must provide audit reports for 3 to 5 years into the past, assuming the system has been in existence for that long.

Next must come the details of the security standing behind the bond. These include indication of whether the issuer is pledging its gross or net revenues toward payment of principal and interest; its proposed flow of funds, that is, the order in which it proposes to pay its bills and obligations; a description of any special funds it has established and their use and purpose; parity provisions, that is, whether any other bonds have equal or greater claims on revenues than the bond in question; the terms of the bond's indenture; a description of any outstanding liens on the project's assets or revenues; and the project's debt service schedules for outstanding issues and the new issue.

Fifth, Standard & Poor's requires details on any other covenants that help protect the property. Thus it wants to know what insurance is carried on or in relation to the project, who is responsible for maintenance and repairs, and whether compulsory audits are required.

Finally, the investment advisory organization requires economic data about the area in which the project will function. Such data must include population trends, income levels, the composition of local industry, and so forth.

Actually, still further information is required. But its nature varies according to the nature of the project.

In the case of an electric system Standard & Poor's demands a description of power capacities and the ways this ower is used; rates and charges, completely broken down; a customer count, both historical and projected; a list of projected large commercial and industrial users; and an indication of the availability of power contracts.

If the project is a water system, the investment advisory organization wants to know the source of the water supply; the historical and projected usage of water; climatic conditions that may affect revenues; the customer count, both historical and projected; the kinds of customers involved and how much each kind is expected to contribute to revenues; a list of industrial users, if any, with indication of how much water they use annually and with whether these amounts are subject to cyclical variations; rates, charges, and fees; the manner in which the water supply is treated; how other systems in the area compare with the one that will be constructed; and, finally, projections of further construction in the future.

In the case of a sewerage system the following information is required: a description of the nature of the system; an indication of what it has been like in the past and what it will be like in the future; an indication of whether users and potential users must be connected with the system; rates and charges; information about the terrain of the area being, or to be, served; a list of contracts with developers in the area; an indication of where and how waste is discharged and of who is responsible for treating it; an indication of the area's water usage; evidence of the area's growth; a customer count; assessments, if any; and evidence of whether federal or state aid will be available to help finance construction of the system.

Parking facilities constitute another kind of project often financed by revenue bonds. Here Standard & Poor's wants a master plan of the area; indication of what other transportation facilities are available into and out of the area; a list of access routes in existence or to be constructed; a traffic count in the area to be served; rates and charges; indication of the availability, if any, of free parking; and a list of nearby shopping facilities.

How Municipal Bonds Are Rated 125

Finally, airports are sometimes financed by revenue bonds. In these cases the airport authority must indicate what area the airport serves; which airlines use it; how many flights there are; what the traffic counts for these flights are or are expected to be; what competition the airport faces; and what revenues it has pledged toward payment of principal and interest. The authority must also provide copies of the agreements that allow various airlines to use the airport.

If you recall the rating definitions given in Chapter 2, you will have a very good idea of the four factors Standard & Poor's considers most important in rating revenue bonds: the level of debt service coverage; the stability of the revenues pledged toward debt service coverage; the bond's basic security provisions; and management. Let us look more closely:

The level of fixed-charge coverage expected of revenue bonds varies somewhat according to the nature of the project. Yet very obviously, no project can hope to have its bonds qualify for a rating of triple-B or higher unless its net revenues at least match its fixed charges.

Otherwise Standard & Poor's insists that it has no immutable standards as to what constitutes adequate coverage. Says Richard Huff:

> We have been asked this question many times, and our answer is always the same. I could cite many examples of comparable projects with comparable fixed-charge coverage. Yet one receives an A+ rating, verging on double-A, while another barely qualifies for a triple-B rating.
>
> Why is this so? One reason is that we're just as concerned with the quality of coverage as with the quantity. For example, the New Jersey Turnpike Authority has never had an excessive amount of fixed-charge coverage. Yet its bonds are rated single-A or better, in part because it is able to increase its tolls whenever necessary to meet its fixed charges and other costs.

All of this brings up the question of how stable pledged revenues are. Obviously, their stability can be affected by a host of matters. A growth or decline in population is one. The overall status of a region's or the nation's economy is another.

Thus a recession can have a particularly devastating effect on airport revenues. This may be particularly true if an airport is heavily dependent on tourist business. Airlines may simply cancel many flights.

Obviously, a project's rates affect its revenues, too. As a result, Standard & Poor's checks whether a given project is charging rates comparable to those of similar facilities in its region. It also checks whether the project can raise rates on its own or whether it must obtain permission from local government or a regulatory commission. Whichever is the case, Standard & Poor's checks whether the project has enjoyed a history of timely rate adjustments. "More and more," says Hyman Grossman, "we are seeing definite lags in rate adjustments. Because of inflation, these lags can clearly affect revenues adversely."

Special factors may also affect revenues, depending on the nature of the project. For example, are we talking about a water-supply system? If so, is it located in an area subject to droughts, hurricanes, or floods? Any one of these natural catastrophes can reduce revenues.

Standard & Poor's investigates all these factors in studying revenue stability. And obviously, if a system has been in operation for a number of years, the investment advisory organization wants to know whether revenues have been stable in the past.

When it turns to a bond's basic security provisions, Standard & Poor's looks into a number of matters. One is whether gross or net revenues are pledged. Standard & Poor's much prefers the latter and, in any case, always analyzes the revenues on a net basis. The point is, operating costs could eat up gross revenues, leaving little or nothing left over.

In what order does the project plan to spend its revenues? The usual order is maintenance costs, debt service, reserve fund, and renewal and replacement of equipment. Reversal of this order may raise questions.

Above and beyond this, Standard & Poor's is concerned with the reserve fund in and of itself. This fund is set up to provide a cushion against the possibility that revenues may not always be sufficient to pay off principal and interest. The investment advisory organization prefers that the amount set aside initially or soon be equal to at least one year's debt service costs.

This in turn brings up the question of what will happen to any surplus the project may earn. Will the project be allowed to keep it, or will the city in which the project is located siphon off the surplus either in whole or in part? There are advantages both ways, but Standard & Poor's at least wants to know what the arrangement will be.

Indenture terms can be important. Of particular concern is the nature of the limitation on issuance of additional bonds in the future. A common provision is that the project must maintain a certain level of debt service coverage before being allowed to sell more debt.

Does the project have any outstanding liens on its revenues? If so, the liens can have an impact on its ability to pay off debt, as can debt service

How Municipal Bonds Are Rated

schedules. If a project has a number of bonds outstanding, it may become overburdened with payments of principal and interest in certain years. Orderly retirement of debt is desired.

Other covenants also play a role in determining whether a bond's basic security provisions are adequate. In this connection the investment advisory organization usually compares similar projects against each other.

In case of fire is there sufficient insurance not only to cover debt service costs but also to pay for rebuilding costs and employee wages? There should be.

Who is responsible for paying the project's maintenance and repair costs? Commonly, the indenture clearly indicates that either the city or the utility will be responsible.

The question in Standard & Poor's mind is whether the responsible party lives up to its obligation. To make sure, the investment advisory organization likes a project to hire an outside consultant every few years to make a survey.

Are the project's accounts subject to compulsory annual audits? They usually are but Standard & Poor's wants to be assured that independent auditors are used.

Finally, the investment advisory organization looks at management. Financial results are one indicator of the quality of management, as is evidence of the ability to plan ahead. And so is evidence of a willingness to raise rates in the face of political pressure not to raise them.

There is one other important point about revenue bonds worth mentioning. It involves so-called moral obligation bonds. This kind of bond is relatively new. In fact, the first appeared less than two decades ago.

It works as follows: Some public authority—perhaps a state housing agency—issues a regular revenue bond. In so doing it seeks and obtains a moral pledge from its parent—usually the state itself—that if its revenues are insufficient to meet its debt service costs, the parent will make up the difference.

This kind of bond is controversial, because the parent is under no legal obligation to rescue the issuer. It is only under a moral obligation to do so. And the moral obligation that one state legislature makes in, say, 1976 may be disregarded by another state legislature 10 years later.

What is Standard & Poor's attitude toward these bonds? In general it is favorably inclined toward them. In fact, its official policy is to rate a moral obligation bond one notch lower than the bonds of the parent who has made the moral obligation.

Exceptions involve projects that seem very strong financially and operationally. These projects' bonds may be given the same ratings as bonds issued by the entities that have undertaken the moral obligations. It is important to understand, however, that Standard & Poor's decisions to give such ratings are based on its appraisals of the issuers, not of the entities that have made the moral guarantees.

Now let us look at how Standard & Poor's recently rated two revenue bonds:

In November 1975 the Los Angeles, California Department of Water and Power issued $50 million worth of revenue bonds, due to mature serially between 1980 and 1999, plus a $25.6 million term bond, due to mature in 2015. The latter bond is subject to sinking fund payments in each of the last 15 years of its life. Both bonds are secured by the power system's revenues. The proceeds from their sales are being used to continue the system's construction program.

In Standard & Poor's opinion, the Department of Water and Power had had a good operating record and was in strong financial condition. Specifically, its net revenues had risen in each of the last 2 years, and it had just won approval for an increase in its electric rates, which was expected to further increase its revenues by about 12 percent annually. Furthermore, its current ratio (assets to liabilities) was up very sharply from the reporting period of 2 years earlier. And although it was likely that the department would issue still more construction bonds, its right to do so is stringently limited by the terms of its indenture. Result: The bonds were rated double-A.

About the same time Homestead, Florida, a small city located some 30 miles southwest of Miami, issued $4 million worth of electric and water revenue bonds, due to mature serially between 1976 and 1999. Among other things, the proceeds from the sale of the bonds are being used to build two new wells and a water-treatment plant.

The bonds are secured by a third lien on the electric and water system's revenues. Bonds that were issued earlier and that are due to reach final maturation in 1984 and 1992, respectively, hold first and second liens.

The customers of both the city's electric and water systems had declined slightly in number from the preceding year. Also, some of the

How Municipal Bonds Are Rated

water system's earnings must be used to correct a massive leakage.

On the other hand, the city's electric system was benefiting from a fuel-adjustment clause that enabled it to pass on rapidly rising fuel costs to its customers. Despite this, both electric and water rates seemed moderate.

Furthermore, said Standard & Poor's, the power system had a satisfactory operating record and satisfactory fixed-charge coverage. Specifically, preliminary 1975 figures showed that revenues available for debt service would cover the system's maximum annual costs between now and 1992 nearly one and one-half times. This coverage factored in the new bonds as well as those already outstanding.

So the investment advisory organization rated the bonds BBB+—one-half notch higher than it had rated earlier third-lien bonds issued by Homestead. It also raised the rating on the city's second-lien bonds from A to A+.

There are two kinds of revenue bonds to which we must now give special attention. We look at one kind very briefly, the other in some depth.

The first kind consists of housing bonds. A few such bonds are guaranteed by the city in which the housing authority that issues the bond is located. They are, therefore, general obligations of the city and are so assessed.

There is a special kind of housing bond that is treated somewhat differently. It is known as a leased housing bond, and it is issued by a local public housing authority. It differs from other housing bonds in that the United States Government promises to make an annual contribution that is at least equal to the bond issuer's annual fixed-charge costs. Thus the issuer is not totally dependent on rental revenues to meet these costs. At least this is the way it works with housing bonds issued under Section 23 of the Housing Act of 1937.

In rating these bonds, Standard & Poor's asks these three questions: Has the local housing authority obtained an approved lease from the Department of Housing and Urban Development (HUD)? Has HUD issued a so-called annual contributions contract guaranteeing to pay the authority a subsidy at least equal to the cost of servicing its debt? And has a separate document been issued assigning this contract to the housing corporation (as opposed to the housing authority) that actually issued the bond?

If the answers to all three questions are yes, Standard & Poor's invariably rates the bond in question double-A. The bond does not qualify for a triple-A rating, because it is not regarded as a direct obligation of the United States Government.

Today, however, no bonds are being issued under Section 23 of the Housing Act. Instead they are being issued under Section 8. And there is a big difference between the two.

Under Section 23, HUD agrees to pay a subsidy tied to all of the units in a housing complex. Under Section 8, it agrees to pay a subsidy tied only to those units that are actually occupied. Obviously, this can mean that the subsidy will not be big enough to cover the issuing corporation's debt service costs.

Standard & Poor's has striven hard to devise a formula for rating these new bonds, and its recommendations are currently being studied by HUD. Until this matter is resolved, the rating agency believes that it cannot rate the bonds because it thinks that the subsidies promised under Section 8 are too speculative in amount. This makes it difficult, if not impossible, to determine how safe principal and interest payments are.

The second kind of revenue bonds to which we must give special attention are hospital bonds. In view of the vast amount of debt constantly issued by states and cities, it may surprise you to learn that rating hospital bonds currently constitutes one of the most active areas in Standard & Poor's municipal bond department.

In the past 8 years, this department has rated more than 325 tax-exempt hospital revenue bonds with a total face value of more than $3.3 billion. Says Richard Huff: "There have been times when we have had a dozen or more hospital bond issues under review, and it is rare when we aren't considering at least two or three of them."

The amount of formal, written information that Standard & Poor's requires from the issuers of hospital bonds is considerable, and the factors that it studies in rating these issues are seemingly endless.

The information includes two copies of the issuer's official statement, which is the equivalent of the prospectus on a corporate bond; a copy of the bond resolution or trust indenture; a copy of the hospital's audits for at least the last 3 years; two copies of its so-called feasibility report, which is usually prepared by an outside accounting or hospital consulting firm and which details the scope of the proposed project, the need for it, its ability to pay its own way, and related matters; a copy of the lease agreement between the hospital and any outside owner; and any perti-

How Municipal Bonds Are Rated

nent miscellaneous matter, such as an architect's report or important newspaper stories about the hospital.

The factors that Standard & Poor's considers in rating hospital bonds fall into 12 categories.

First, it wants to know something about the history of the hospital, assuming it is not brand-new. When was it established? Has it ever expanded before and, if so, in what way? What are its existing facilities? What services are provided? What are its medical and nursing school affiliations, if any?

"The answers to these questions rarely reflect either favorably or unfavorably on a hosptial," observes Huff. "But they do enable us to see it in total context and compare it with other hospitals."

Second, Standard & Poor's wants to know about the expansion program itself. What exactly is being built? Why is it needed? Are existing hospital beds merely being replaced, or are they being upgraded? What about ancillary services? Are they being replaced, upgraded, or established for the very first time? Finally, what is the nature of the construction contract?

Much of this information is contained in the feasibility report. Says Huff: "We are particularly interested in two points. First, what is the hospital's bed occupancy rate? Obviously, we would usually question the wisdom of installing more beds if the occupancy rate were only 60 or 65 percent. Second, who is the contractor? What is his reputation and experience? Did he have to bid to win the contract? Has he put up a completion bond? We like hospitals to require bids and bonds."

Next, Standard & Poor's looks at various technical provisions affecting the bond. These include the hospital's lease and mortgage, if any; its debt maturity schedule; its rate covenant, that is, its promise to charge rates sufficient to return enough revenue to provide some coverage of its debt service costs; its debt service reserve; its additional reserves; the terms governing its right to issue additional bonds; its flow of funds, including its provisions for funding depreciation; its insurance; and its pledge of gross or net revenues toward payment of its debt. As in the case of other revenue bonds, Standard & Poor's likes orderly retirement of debt, some reserve against a rainy day, some limitation on the right to issue additional debt, and a pledge of net rather than gross revenues.

One other question in this area is of importance. Does the hospital retain an independent consultant to review its finances and operations on a regular or a periodic basis? It is a good sign if it does.

Standard & Poor's also wants to learn about the entire area that the hospital serves. How big is the area? What is its economic base? What are the size, composition, and typical educational and income levels of its population? What is the hospital's position in the area? How many competing hospitals are there? What are their occupancy rates? Do they have plans to expand?

Richard Huff says one of the most important areas to investigate is management. Standard & Poor's wants to know who the hospital's trustees are, what their experience is, how they were chosen, how active they have been, and what they expect of the hospital. It asks much the same questions about the administrative staff, dipping down to the department level. It also wants to know the relationship of both these groups to the professional staff.

A critical question involves management's ability to manage. How well does it plan for the future? How well does it staff? How effective are its efforts to control costs and to collect on its bills? How do its financial results compare with its budget estimates?

"You can often get a good line on management," says Huff, "by checking its financial results during a period of stress—say, when price controls are in effect or when doctors are on strike. I know of two hospitals in California, both of which suffered from strikes lasting several months. One's professional staffing procedures were so flexible that it lost only $2,000. The other's were so inflexible that it lost $800,000."

In this connection there has been a rise in recent years in consulting firms that manage hospitals for a fee. "You won't find such consultants at a hospital like Chicago's Rush-Presbyterian," says Huff, "because its administrative staff has such great depth. But they can sometimes be useful in a new hospital or a small one unable to attract top-flight people. Generally, we're favorably inclined toward these consultants, although we're very aware that some are not as good as others. But regardless of the quality of a consultant, we always want to know its philosophy of management."

The professional staff is also closely investigated. Who are its members? How old are they? Where are they located in relation to the hospital? What specialties do they represent? How many are board certified or board eligible? How many have come into the area recently—and how many have left? Were those still there formally queried on their opinions about the quality of the hospital, its need for expansion, and the likelihood that they would use the facilities that will be constructed?

Not surprisingly, Standard & Poor's also checks the hospital's occupancy and utilization rates, on both an inpatient and outpatient basis. It wants to know the projected rates as well.

The investment advisory organization even checks the length of the average hospital stay. Typically, hospitals earn most of their income during the first few days patients are hospitalized, when most diagnostic tests are made. Therefore, if the average stay can be reduced even one day, a hospital will increase its income.

Is the hospital accredited? Have its construction plans been approved by a regional hospital planning agency and by appropriate state agencies? What powers do these agencies have to enforce their edicts? These questions are asked, too.

Standard & Poor's also looks at the hospital's third-party payors and the relative amounts each kind contributes to revenues. It is wary of hospitals that are heavily dependent on Medicare and Medicaid payments. The latter's rates of reimbursement are lower than those of commercial insurance companies. It is also wary of hospitals that are located in states having budgetary problems. These states may cut back on their Medicaid payments.

Are municipal taxes levied to support the hospital? Is it endowed and, if so, by how much? What kind of volunteer programs does it have, and how effective are they? Does it benefit from fund-raising drives, and if so, do they represent continuing or sporadic efforts? Any evidence of strong community support is a plus.

Next, Standard & Poor's wants to know the hospital's revenues and earnings for the past 5 years and what it is estimated that they will be for the next 5 years. Naturally, it compares the earnings of comparable hospitals and, other things being equal, likes earnings to be consistent. "Earnings that bounce around from year to year can be a bad sign," says Huff.

In this connection the investment advisory organization looks at accounts receivable. A hospital that collects on its accounts in fewer than 50 days is doing a good job, Huff avers. One that collects within 70 days is doing a normal job. But one that takes 90 days or more is probably not as efficient as it could be, although there may be a reason for its record. Some Blue Cross plans, for example, are notoriously slow payors.

By the same token, a hospital that is unable to collect on 7 percent or more of its accounts receivable raises eyebrows. The typical hospital is able to collect on all but 2 to 5 percent, says Huff.

Again, what do debt service costs amount to in relation to gross revenues? The lower the percentage, the better. In this regard 6 percent is considered low, 10 percent typical, 15 percent high.

As in the case of other revenue bonds, Standard & Poor's has no fixed guidelines as to what constitutes adequate fixed-charge coverage. But obviously, a hospital whose earnings do not at least match its fixed-charge costs has very little chance of receiving a rating of triple-B or higher.

Finally, Standard & poor's turns its attention to the hospital's balance sheet. What is the hospital's equity in relation to its debt? A 50-50 ratio is usually considered good.

How much of the money being raised for construction will be provided by the bond issue? It is a good sign if a hospital is providing a substantial amount from surplus funds, from a fund-raising drive, or from both.

How much working capital does the hospital have? This is not usually a problem with an established institution, but it can prove a difficulty with one just starting up. The way to check is to ascertain the hospital's current ratio, that is, its ratio of current assets to current liabilities. Standard & Poor's likes a ratio of three to one. And it is apt to be concerned if the ratio is less than one and one-half to one.

What is the balance of the hospital's funds, that is, the portion of equity on its balance sheet? Over a period of time even a nonprofit hospital should generate some surplus, if only through bequests and other gifts.

As you can see, rating hospital bonds is an exhaustive job. But of all the factors Standard & Poor's considers, three are paramount: What is the hospital's competitive position in its area? How strong is its medical staff? How good is its management?

The last factor is so important that Standard & Poor's municipal bond analysts probably do more traveling to rate hospital bonds than any other kind. Says Huff: "It's very difficult for us to get an adequate impression of a hospital and its environment without meeting some of the people. We like to talk with representatives of both the trustees and the administration, with the feasibility consultant, with the underwriter, and possibly with the bond attorney. If time permits, we prefer to hold these meetings at the hospital itself."

How Municipal Bonds Are Rated

Where does it all lead? Only a handful of hospital bonds, such as those issued by institutions like Boston's Massachusetts General Hospital and Detroit's Henry Ford Hospital, are rated as high as double-A. The great bulk are rated either single-A or triple-B. Hospitals are more likely to get the lower of these two ratings if they are just starting up, relocating, or expanding to a very substantial degree, or if they have become subject to very stiff competition.

One other matter is of note: Because of the many factors that must be considered in weighing a hospital bond, the time this takes, and the travel that is frequently involved, Standard & Poor's fee for rating such bonds is somewhat higher than it is for most other municipal issues. This fee usually ranges from $1500 to $2500 and is sometimes even higher.

Finally, we must touch briefly on a relatively new development in the municipal bond field. In very recent years two different organizations—one an association of four insurance companies, the other an insurance corporation—have begun insuring certain municipal bonds, thus guaranteeing that their principal and interest payments will be made on time. These may be either general obligation or revenue bonds.

In part because this new kind of insurance can substantially reduce the amount of interest that must be paid on bonds, it is likely to be used more and more frequently. Yet there will probably be a limit on its growth. This is partly because one of the organizations does not insure any issues whose face value exceeds $20 million.

What tack does Standard & Poor's take toward these insured bonds?

In the case of one organization, it makes sure that the issue at least merits a rating of triple-B. If so, it gives the issue, if subsequently insured, a rating of double-A.

In the case of the other organization, Standard & Poor's does not study the individual issues insured, although it does monitor their overall quality. If the issues are insured, the investment advisory organization gives them a rating of triple-A.

The fact that Standard & Poor's gives the bonds insured by one organization a rating of double-A and those rated by the other organization a rating of triple-A is based on its estimate of the financial and other strengths of the insurers, not those of the issuers.

How To Get A Better Rating For Your Bonds   14

How can your company, state, city, public authority—or, if you represent a foreign country, national government—obtain a better rating for its bonds? There is no easy answer to that question. In fact, there may be no answer at all.

As we have seen, Standard & Poor's tries to probe almost every facet of the operations of any organization whose bonds it rates. As we have also seen, an organization's statistics—its ratio of debt to working capital, for example—tell a great deal about it and usually play an important role in the rating its bonds receive. If the numbers, as Standard & Poor's analysts refer to these statistics, are unfavorable, there may be little or nothing that can be done to obtain a good rating.

Yet, although the numbers are important, they are rarely all-important. Other factors, such as the quality of an organization's management and its future plans, are given great weight.

Beyond that, the investment advisory organization's analysts are quick to acknowledge that they are human. The fact that they allow corporations and other organizations to appeal the ratings that are given their bond issues is further proof that the rating process is never so cut-and-dried as to preclude every effort to put your best foot forward.

What precisely can you do? Here are some tips specifically aimed at corporations, although most apply to governments and governmental bodies, too.

First, apply for a rating early. Give Standard & Poor's at least a month to study your written material. If you can allow an additional 2 weeks, so much the better. The investment advisory organization will probably want to talk with your management either in New York City or on its home grounds.

In fact, if your company issues bonds only occasionally and has not issued any in some time, you may do well to approach Standard & Poor's before you register the proposed issue with the SEC. If you do so, the investment advisory organization will be able to give the bond a preliminary rating. If the rating is not satisfactory, you can reweigh your plans in light of its decision.

Perhaps you will want to drop your plans altogether, or perhaps you will want to try to place the bond issue privately. In either case Standard & Poor's preliminary rating will never be publicized.

Once you register your proposed issue with the SEC, the matter will be out of your hands. Standard & Poor's rates all industrial, utility, and certain other kinds of corporate bonds that have been registered with the SEC whether it is asked to do so or not. It publishes these ratings, too. It believes that in so doing it is acting in the public interest.

Second, work closely with the investment bank that is planning to underwrite your issue. It knows or should know the kind and amount of information that Standard & Poor's wants and be able to advise you on your entire presentation.

Third, provide all the documentary material that Standard & Poor's requests. If there is a question as to just what is wanted, err on the side of providing too much information rather than too little.

In each chapter in this book dealing with particular kinds of bonds, I have indicated the minimum amount of information that the agency seeks. In the appendix immediately following this chapter, I have indicated a desirable manner of presenting this information. (There is nothing comparable for municipalities because the nature of their reports and even the terminology they use vary so much from issuer to issuer.)

Adds Roy Weinberger, one of the managers of the agency's corporate finance department: "Multi-market companies or companies with numerous subsidiaries in different businesses should provide us with consolidating financial statements. It is difficult enough to assess a company with just one or two divisions, let alone one with 20 or 30, without knowing how each segment of the business is doing, how it is capitalized, and so forth."

Fourth, bring the right people to any meeting with Standard & Poor's analysts. The investment advisory organization likes to see executives who can effectively cover three facets of corporate activities—finances, operations, and philosophy. This argues for a person or persons at least at the vice presidential level.

Occasionally, one person can handle the job satisfactorily, but it is usually better to send more than one. Otherwise Standard & Poor's will wonder what the rest of management is like. And as you know, its assessment of management plays an important role in its ratings.

Two executives can sometimes do the job. But three or four are usually better. If you decide to send more than four, you had better have a very good idea of what and how much each will contribute to the meeting.

Fifth, bring along a representative of your investment banking firm if you like. Especially if your firm is inexperienced in the debt market, he may help keep the talks on target.

Sixth, avoid one-man shows like the plague. Analyst after analyst I have talked with indicates that this is one of the most common mistakes made by corporations. Explains Kenneth Alterman, another manager in Standard & Poor's corporate finance department:

Occasionally, a company president will come into our offices with four or five other executives. Often we find that only the president answers our questions. If any of the other executives try to answer, he cuts them off. Or if he lets them answer, they direct their answers to him rather than to us.

This usually indicates that management is not a team and has no real depth. If the president dies, retires, or leaves the company, it may encounter serious problems.

Next, anticipate Standard & Poor's questions. There's no point in rehashing your annual report or your registration statement. The analysts will already have reviewed them.

You will do better to concentrate on the problems your company faces. As Roy Weinberger puts it: "It is far preferable that you bring your problems to our attention—and describe your plans for solving them —than leave it to us to bring them up."

It almost goes without saying that you should be frank in making your presentation and in answering any questions the analysts may have. If you are tempted to err on the side of caution, remember three things:

First, as a matter of course, Standard & Poor's analysts probe the negatives in any company's activities. But just because they seem to concentrate on the negative, do not automatically assume that they are reaching negative conclusions about your company.

Second, do not assume that you are expected to answer particular questions in a particular way. All that is required is that you provide enough detail for the analysts to understand the answers. "Also," adds Kenneth Alterman, "remember that often it is not so much the specific answer an executive gives that counts, but his thought process and depth of reasoning."

Third, bear in mind that any information you proffer is given in confidence. Standard & Poor's corporate bond analysts do not share the information they obtain with any employees outside of the corporate finance department.

In making your presentation, employ meaningful comparisons. Most executives who talk with Standard & Poor's analysts like to emphasize how they think their companies stack up against other corporations. In making such comparisons, you can help your company put its best foot forward and also help the analysts make their assessment. Just be sure that you compare apples with apples. Otherwise your efforts may go to waste or even redound against you.

Says Weinberger: "Over the years I've seen all kinds of comparisons made. Some executives have even compared manufacturing companies with finance companies or with utilities. Such comparisons are of little or no value to us. What we're interested in is how a company stacks up against its direct competitors or other companies that share common characteristics with it."

Never forget to discuss your plans for the future. In making your written presentation, you should, if at all possible, make projections of your sales, earnings, cash flow, and so forth. Ordinarily, Standard & Poor's likes to see such projections for 5 years into the future, although it is quick to admit that, the further ahead they are made, the more tentative they must be.

How To Get A Better Rating For Your Bonds

Even if you provide the investment advisory organization with projections, it will inquire into your future plans. Emphasizes Juliette Gould, another manager in the agency's corporate finance department: "We are not impressed with a company that has few or no plans. We want to know where a company wants to go and how it hopes to get there.

"For example, we may inquire about a company's philosophy about acquisitions. We always trust it has one. We're apt to have reservations about a firm that says: We'll deal with that problem if and when it arises."

Next, limit your oral presentation to 15 or 30 minutes. Stress the highlights and strong points of your activities. But leave time for the analysts' questions. No matter how much you have tried to anticipate their queries, they are bound to have more. Often, answering these queries will take up another hour or hour and one-half of time.

Do not hesitate to appeal the rating your bond issue is given if you believe that it is not high enough. Once Standard & Poor's decides on a rating, it so informs the investment banker that is planning to underwrite the issue. In so doing, it not only indicates what the rating will be, but also lists the issuer's strengths and weaknesses as it sees them.

In appealing a rating, you should certainly concentrate on the weaknesses that Standard & Poor's perceives. But do not hesitate to bring up strengths that you believe may not have been given sufficient weight. It is true that most companies don't appeal. It is also true that, of those that do, a majority fail to effect a change.

Nonetheless, a noticeable minority do effect a change. So this course may be worthwhile if you truly believe that an injustice has been done. Just bear in mind that the most common reason why Standard & Poor's changes a preliminary rating is that the corporation (or municipality) in question provides it with important information it had not previously disclosed.

Another way of looking at this possibility is to remember the value of preventive medicine. Disclose enough about your company in the first place so that a fair assessment is possible, and you will not have to go back to seek a change.

Finally, make annual follow-ups on your rating. This should be done even if you are not planning to issue any more debt in the near future.

As we have seen, the investment advisory organization usually reviews all corporate and municipal ratings annually. As we have also seen, it ordinarily expects the issuers to keep it provided with annual and interim reports and other data clearly pertinent to their operations.

Despite this, Standard & Poor's advises that some representative of your company come in approximately once a year to provide an update. Says Weinberger: "We appreciate this kind of periodic contact. More important, it helps to avoid surprises. As you may guess, the worst thing that a debt issuer can do is to surprise a rating agency."

As I indicated earlier, virtually all the advice concerning corporations applies equally well to governmental bodies on every level. Yet a few points deserve special emphasis, and a couple of more must be added.

Do provide Standard & Poor's with enough time to rate an issue. "Municipalities are spoiled," says Hyman C. Grossman, a vice president in the municipal bond department. "We often get requests to rate an issue only 3 or 4 days before it is to be sold. This might have been all right a decade ago. It is not all right now. Where we once took hours to rate an issue, we may now take days."

Choose your underwriter with care. And do not assume that all the best ones are located in New York or Chicago. Indeed, some located there are of less than top-flight quality. What's more, there are some good regional firms.

The problem is, some municipal bond issuers choose their underwriters partly on a political basis. Sometimes the underwriters just are not prepared to answer Standard & Poor's questions. Says Richard E. Huff, another vice president in the municipal bond department:

> Just the other day an underwriter representing a school district visited us in search of a rating. He didn't bring along the district's budget and didn't know what was in it.
>
> Obviously, a budget is very important to the rating process. And when we run into situations like this, where we can't resolve important questions in our minds, a less than satisfactory rating often results.

Provide enough information right from the start. In a certain sense issuers of municipal bonds are handicapped in this regard. Unlike corporate issuers, they do not have to file their offerings and pertinent information about themselves with the SEC. As a result, they do not always provide Standard & Poor's with enough information either.

Curiously, states tend to be worse offenders than major cities do. The former have plenty of information that could give Standard & Poor's

How To Get A Better Rating For Your Bonds

fuller and more favorable pictures of themselves, but they do not bother to forward it. For example, in seeking a rating not long ago, one Western state sent in a brief two-page memo. Nothing more.

"By contrast," says John K. Pfeiffer, vice president of Standard & Poor's bond division, "North Carolina does a superb job of providing information on both the state and local level."

A major reason is that some years ago the state set up a local government commission. Now all bonds issued by or in the state must be approved by this commission, which makes sure that every unit in the state supplies sufficient information to Standard & Poor's and other rating agencies.

You will do well, adds Hyman Grossman, to provide such information to major institutional investors as well. It may help sell your bonds.

Provide follow-up information. At the very least, you should provide Standard & Poor's with audited financial statements.

Many issuers of municipal bonds do not do so. The issuers of general obligation bonds are particularly lax in this regard. In fact, Standard & Poor's has become so concerned about the problem that, late in 1975, it wrote to a sizable number of municipal bond issuers warning them that, unless they forwarded financial statements within 30 days, it would be forced to withdraw its ratings on their bonds outstanding.

There seems little more to say. The rating agencies have become quasi-public bodies. The ratings they give usually have a direct impact on the amount of interest that issuing corporations and governmental bodies must pay. And sometimes they even affect the issuers' ability to sell the bonds. Anything you can do to tell your organization's story as fully as possible is likely to help, if only because it will make your organization stand out from the herd.

Appendix
Introduction to Appendix

The following written material and exhibits are designed to help corporations seeking ratings for their bonds and other securities to present information about themselves in an organized, readily usable manner. Although Standard & Poor's does not require that the information be presented in this fashion, it does consider the method an excellent one.

Both the written material and the exhibits were prepared by the corporate financial counseling department of Irving Trust Company of New York and published by that company, in copyright form, in a booklet entitled *The Rating of Corporate Debt Issues.* I am indebted to Irving Trust Company for allowing me to reproduce the material, which I have done with only a few slight stylistic changes.

What to Include

1. Brief description of the offering
   Indicate type of instrument, size of issue, interest rate, maturity, plus sinking fund and redemption provisions, if applicable.

2. Use of proceeds
   State the intended use(s) of the proceeds of the financing. If there is more than one, list each use, plus its dollar amount and the percen-

tage of the total. Classifications such as working capital or general funds can be used where applicable; however, any single sizable expenditure should be specifically noted and treated separately.
3. Effect of offering on capitalization

	As of ____, 19____		Adjusted for proposed offering	
Short-term debt and long-term debt due within 1 year (if applicable)	$ _____		$ _____	
Long-term capital	$	%	$	%
Long-term debt (in order of seniority)				
Preferred stock				
Common equity	_____		_____	
Total long-term capital	_____	____%	_____	____%

*If you are applying for a commercial paper rating, list each type of short-term debt separately.

4. Description of the company and its policies
   A. General history—a brief discussion of the company's evolution and of what it currently does, e.g., manufactures, sells at retail, and services household appliances, including washing machines, dryers, and refrigerators.
   B. Corporate goals—a statement of the corporation's overall quantitative and/or qualitative goals, e.g., earn 10 percent on equity, be the second largest manufacturer of playpens in the state; plus an outline of the plans formulated to achieve these goals, e.g., acquisitions, cost-reduction program.
   C. Corporate structure—a simplified organization chart depicting the various divisions or departments. This can be supplemented by text.
   D. Corporate director and management
      1. List directors and their affiliations.
      2. Management—Include names, titles, ages, and responsibilities of top management. Provide information on the decision-making structure, e.g., centralized versus decentralized, level at which specific decisions are made.
   E. Description of products or market groups
      1. Outline in detail what the company does or makes and what

Appendix

each subsidiary (division) does. And provide anything that will help pinpoint the various products (pictures, brand names, etc.)
2. Provide in exhibit form (See Exhibit 2) a breakout of each product's or market group's contribution to sales and profits. Any factor that has had or is expected to have a particularly significant effect on sales or profits should be thoroughly explained, e.g., a revolutionary new process. The effects can be illustrated in chart form.

F. Marketing—List the particular segments of the market that the company competes in and its major competitors in each. Include such data as market share, market's historical growth, and trends within these areas of specialization. Outline management's plans for increasing market share, if applicable.

G. Financial policies and controls
1, The company's general financial policies (capital structure policy and dividend policy) should be outlined.
2. A brief discussion of any internal budgeting and planning system(s), the financial standards used to judge management's performance, and any intersubsidiary or interdivisional financial arrangements, e.g., each subsidiary must remit 75 percent of pretax profit to the parent, should also be included.

5. Financial review
A. Summarize your accounting procedure and the methods used in calculating the financial relationships included in the schedules. These relationships should be computed by using the same formulas that Standard & Poor's uses (see Exhibit 1). Also, if there is any account peculiar to the industry that has a significant effect on the industry, it should be defined and explained.
B. Historical data—5 years are probably sufficient; however, 10 years are preferable. Where acquisitions are significant, both reported *and* restated sales and net income figures should be shown.
C. Projected figures—Include for 5 years and, in the case of commercial paper ratings, for 3 years. List all assumptions and their basis, i.e., historical average, management estimates, etc.
D. Discuss the company's financing plans. In particular, highlight how the current financing fits into these plans and, if applicable, indicate how the future financing needs indicated in the 5-year or 3-year forecast will likely be met. All these plans should be discussed in relation to the financial policies and goals of the corporation.
E. The following statements should be included:
Income statement (historical and projected)   Exhibit 3
Balance sheet (historical and projected)   Exhibit 4

Comparative data (historical and projected)   Exhibit 5
Changes in financial condition
  (historical and projected)   Exhibit 6
Capitalization (historical and projected)   Exhibit 7
Long-term debt repayment schedule   Exhibit 8
Guarantees and contingent liabilities   Exhibit 9
Schedule of lease obligations   Exhibit 10
Schedule of existing bank lines   Exhibit 11

6. Summary of terms (Exhibit 12)
  A. Include all pertinent facts relating to the issue.
  B. Treat in detail any peculiarities of the issue.

Exhibit 1

Standard & Poor's Formulas for Calculating Various Financial Relationships for Industrial Companies

Fixed-charge coverage

After-tax interest coverage
Including rentals

$$\frac{\text{Total interest charges + adjusted net income*}}{\text{Total interest charges}}$$

$$\frac{\text{Total interest charges + total rentals + adjusted net income*}}{\text{Total interest charges + total rentals}}$$

$\frac{\text{Net tangible assets}}{\text{Long-term debt}}$

$$\frac{\text{Net plant + net working capital + other tangible assets—all deferred charges and reserves on liabilities side}}{\text{Long-term debt (excluding current portions)}}$$

Liquidity ratios

Working capital ratio

$$\frac{\text{Current assets—current liabilities}}{\text{Long-term debt}}$$

Cash flow ratio

$$\frac{\text{Adjusted net income* + depreciation}}{\text{Current liabilities}}$$

Quick ratio (acid test)

$$\frac{\text{Cash + marketable securities + current receivables}}{\text{Current liabilities}}$$

Returns

Return on equity

$$\frac{\text{Adjusted net income*}}{\text{Stockholders' equity}}$$

Return on total assets

$$\frac{\text{Pretax income + total interest charges}}{\text{Total assets}}$$

*This figure should be adjusted for minority interest, equity in undistributed earnings of unconsolidated subsidiaries, and nonrecurring items.

**Sample Format for Presentation
of Corporate Information
to Standard & Poor's**

Name of Company

**Information Prepared for Purposes of Obtaining a Rating
Date:**

This material is *confidential** and was prepared solely for the purpose of obtaining a rating from Standard & Poor's Corp.

*Each page should be stamped: CONFIDENTIAL—FOR RATING PURPOSES ONLY.

Exhibit 2

Name of Company

Contribution to Sales and Profits
(Dollars in thousands)

Year ending (month and day)	Net sales						Profit contribution					
	19__ $ %	19__ $ %	19__ $ %	19__ $ %	19__ $ %	19__ $ %	19__ $ %	19__ $ %	19__ $ %	19__ $ %	19__ $ %	19__ $ %
Product or market group (list)												
Total	=100%	=100%	=100%	=100%	=100%	=100%	=100%	=100%	=100%	=100%	=100%	=100%
Less												
Corporate expenses												
Other unallocated expenses												
Interest												
Taxes							—	—	—	—	—	—
Net income							=	=	=	=	=	=

Exhibit 3

Name of Company

Historical and Project Consolidated Statement of Income
(Dollars in thousands)

	December 31				
	19__	19__	19__	19__	19__
Sales					
Cost of goods sold (if applicable)*					
Gross margin					
Selling and advertising expense					
Depreciation and depletion					
Administrative and general expenses					
Research and development					
Interest on funded debt					
Other interest					
Other expenses (classify if material)					
Taxes other than federal income tax					
Net income before federal income taxes and extraordinary items					
Federal income taxes†					
Net income before extraordinary items					
Extraordinary items (describe the specific items)					
Net income					
Operating margin					
Number of shares used for per share calculation‡					
Earnings per share‡					
Dividends per share‡					
Return on total assets§					
Return on common equity§					

*If the company uses this account, its exact composition must be outlined in detail so that the analyst can clearly differentiate between this account and the remaining expense accounts on the income statement.

†Distinguish between current and deferred income taxes. Disclose treatment and amount of investment tax credit and tax-loss carry-forward credit, if applicable.

‡This figure should be adjusted for stock splits and stock dividends.

§See Exhibit 1 for a definition of this relationship.

Exhibit 4

Name of Company

Historical and Projected Consolidated Balance Sheet
(Dollars in thousands)

	December 31				
	19__	19__	19__	19__	19__
Assets					
Current assets*					
Investments					
Property, plant and equipment accumulated depreciation					
Property, plant and equipment (net)					
Other tangible assets					
Intangible assets†					
Total					
Liabilities and stockholders' equity					
Current liabilities*					
Long-term debt (less current portion shown above)					
Other liabilities					
Stockholders' equity					

Quick ratio:†
Current ratio:
Receivables turnover:
Inventory turnover:
Short-term debt/current assets:
Short-term-debt/current liabilities:
Working capital ratio:†
Net tangible assets/total long-term debt:†

*These should be broken down by specific account.
†See Exhibit 1 for a definition of this relationship.

Exhibit 5

Name of Company

Historical and Projected Comparative Data
(Dollars in thousands)

	December 31				
	19__	19__	19__	19__	19__
Net income before taxes					
Net income					
Total interest					
Interest coverage*					
Before tax					
After tax					
Interest and rental coverage*					
Before tax					
After tax					
Depreciation					
Other noncash items					
Cash flow/current liabilities*					
Cash flow/total long-term debt					
Total long-term debt/net plant					
Net tangible assets/total long-term debt*					

*See Exhibit 1 for a definition of this relationship.

Exhibit 6

Name of Company

Historical and Projected Consolidated Statements of Changes in Financial Position
(Dollars in thousands)

	December 31				
	19__	19__	19__	19__	19__
Sources of funds					
Total					
Application of funds					
Total					
Required/excess funds as projected					

Exhibit 7

Name of Company

Historical and Projected Capitalization
(Dollars in thousands)

	December 31				
	19__	19__	19__	19__	19__
Short-term debt*	$____	$____	$____	$____	$____
Long-term debt	$ %	$ %	$ %	$ %	$ %
Preferred stock†					
Common stock and surplus					
Total long-term capital	$__100%	$__100%	$__100%	$__100%	$__100%
Total long-term debt/total long-term capital					
Total debt/total long-term capital plus short-term debt					

*This should include the current portion of long-term debt. And if the presentation is for the purpose of obtaining a rating on commercial paper, short-term debt must be listed by type.
†The liquidating value of these shares should be indicated in a footnote.

155

Exhibit 8
Schedule of Long-Term Debt*
(Dollars in thousands)

Existing	Year-end before proposed issue	Retirement				
		19__	19__	19__	19__	19__
Description (mortgage notes, etc.)						
Subtotals	_____	____	____	____	____	____
Proposed issue						
Totals	_____	____	____	____	____	____
Ending balances						
Less current portion						
Net ending balances	_____	====	====	====	====	====
Total interest expense						

*As a continuation of the schedule, provide the following information on each of the company's existing long-term debt obligations: interest rate and final maturity; source of the financing; major protective covenants.

Exhibit 9

Name of Company

Guarantees and Contingent Liabilities
(Dollars in thousands)

Guarantees

Borrower	Type of Loan	Term of Guarantee	Amount of Guarantee
Total guarantees			

Contingent liabilities

Borrower	Type of Loan	Term of Guarantee	Amount of contingent liability
Total contingent liabilities			
Total guarantees and contingent liabilities			

Exhibit 10

Schedule of Lease Obligations
(Dollars in thousands)

Finance leases*

Type of asset leased	Minimum Annual Rental Payments				Next 5-Year Period	Next 5-Year Period
	19__	19__	19__	19__		
List groups if appropriate	___	___	___	___	___	___
Total	___	___	___	___	___	___

Present value of finance leases:
Average interest rate used to compute present value:

Other leases†

	Minimum Annual Rental Payments		Next 5-Year Period	Next 5-Year Period
Type of asset leased	19__	19__		
List groups if appropriate	___	___	___	___
Total	___	___	___	___

*Long-term noncancelable leases whose original term constitutes 75 percent or more of the useful life of the underlying asset.
†Cancelable leases and noncancelable leases whose original term does not constitute a significant portion of the useful life of the underlying asset.

Exhibit 11

Name of Company

Schedule of Bank Lines*
(Dollars in thousands)

Bank	Name and telephone number of two contacts	Total amount available and rate	Unused portion	Expiration date of agreement (if applicable)

*This information is very important to commercial paper ratings.

Exhibit 12

Name of Company

Summary of Terms
Type of Issue

Dated:
Principal amount:*
Interest rate:
Interest payable:
Maturity:
Form:
Commercial paper dealer(s):
Redemption (when applicable):
   General
   Nonrefundable
   Sinking fund
   Average life
   Delayed delivery arrangements
Covenants:
Modification or amendment of indenture:
Trustee:
Definitions:

*If you are applying for a commercial paper rating, include not only the size of the present issue, but also the anticipated maximum amount that will be outstanding during the next year and the estimated average amount that will be outstanding during the year.

Index

Acquisitions, 29, 36, 78, 85, 113, 141
Airline bonds:
    fixed-charged coverage of, 55, 61, 64
    indentures of, 62-63
    see also Airlines
Airlines:
    asset protection of, 63
    earning power of, 55, 63-64
    financial resources of, 63
    information required of, 62
    management of, 63-64
    see also Airline bonds; *and listings for individual airlines*
Airports, 125
Alterman, Kenneth M., ix, 139, 140
Amos, William W., 90
AMP, 90
Anatomy of the Secondary Market in Corporate Bonds, The, 12n
Appalachian Power, 53
Appendix, 145-158
    references to, 28, 138
Assets:
    current, 31, 32
    definition of net tangible, 28
Australia, 104
Austria, 104

Bank bonds:
    fixed-charge coverage of, 76
    indentures of, 74
    see also Banks, commercial
Banks:
    commercial:
        assets of, 67, 68, 69, 74, 75, 76
        earning power of, 76, 77, 78
        financial resources of, 74-76
        information required of, 66
        letters of credit of, 112
        management of, 69, 77
        see also Bank bonds
    investment, 90, 115
        quality of, 142
        value of, 27, 138, 139
Bankruptcy, 29, 45, 103. *See also* Default
Boatman's Bancshares, 78
Boatmen's National Bank of St. Louis, 78
Bonds:
    definitions of, 9, 48
    limitation on life of, 29n
    prices of, 11
    registration of, 27, 115, 138, 139, 142
    unrated, 13, 19, 21, 25
    see also listings for various kinds of bonds; e.g., Utility bonds

159

Bond Guide, The, 21
Bray, Edward C., ix, 79, 83, 84
Burlington Northern, 61
Business Week, 1, 2, 3

Cash flow:
  definition of, 34
  projections of, 35-36, 140
California, 132
Canada, 100
Certificates of deposit, 67, 70n
Chicago, 67
Civil Aeronautics Board, 61-62, 64
C.I.T. Financial, 86-87
Collateral-trust bonds, 58
Commercial Credit, 86
Commercial paper, 67, 68, 84-85
  bank, 65
  dealers, 110, 113-114
  definitions of, 9, 109
  fixed-charge coverage of, 113
  railroad, 49
  rollover of, 109, 112
  see also Commercial paper issuers
Commercial paper issuers:
  asset protection of, 112
  earning power of, 15, 111, 112, 113, 114
  financial resources of, 14-15, 112
  information required of, 110-111
  management of, 15, 111, 113
  see also Commercial paper
Conservationists, 51
Control Data, 86
Convertible bonds, 39, 41-42, 45, 61
Corcoran, Jerome C., ix, 62, 63, 64
Currencies, foreign:
  payment in, 100
  stability of, 106
  trading in, 76

Dallas, 122
Dayton Hudson, 114
Debt:
  analysis of bank, 69
  growth in, 1, 2
  retirement of, 29, 117-118
  short-term, 33, 49n, 67, 101, 118, 121. *See also* Commercial paper
Default, 4, 12, 16, 18, 19, 29n, 57, 103, 118. *See also* Bankruptcy
De Luca, Rosemary, ix
Depression, The Great, 57
Di Palma, Dominick G., ix, 56, 58, 60
Dow Jones Co., 25
du Pont, 40

Electric systems, 124, 128
Energy crisis, 59
England, 103
Equipment-trust certificates:
  airline, 55, 61, 62
  railroad, 55, 57, 58, 62
Equity, stockholders', 63, 112
Euromarket, vi, 100, 104
Europe, 104
  Eastern, 103
European Coal & Steel Community, 99

Federal funds, 68, 70n
Federal Housing Administration, 92
Federated Department Stores, 36-37
Fees, for rating:
  corporate bonds, 23
  commercial paper, 24
  foreign bonds, 106-107
  hospital bonds, 135
  municipal bonds, 26
  preliminary issues, 23-24
  private placements, 44
  utility bonds, 23
Fendrich, Thomas G., ix, 49, 52, 54
Finance bonds:
  fixed-charge coverage of, 83
  indentures of, 80, 86
  see also Finance companies
Finance companies:
  assets of, 79, 80, 81, 87
  capital structure of, 83-85, 87
  captive companies of, 83, 85-86
  commercial finance companies, 79, 82, 87, 97
  consumer finance companies, 79, 82, 84, 86, 87, 97
  equipment-leasing companies, 84
  factors, 74, 84
  income protection of, 82-83
  information required of, 80
  leasing companies, 79
  management of, 85, 87

Index

personal loan companies, 79
portfolios of, 80-82, 87
sales finance companies, 79
subsidiaries of, 86
see also Finance bonds
Financial statements:
   consolidating, 139
   see also "information required of"
     under listings for various kinds
     of companies
First Boston Corp., The, 90
Fitch Investors Service Inc., v
Fixed-charge coverage:
   definition of, 35
   see also listings under various kinds
     of debt, e.g., Utility bonds
Fixed Income Investor, The, vi, 21, 25
Florida East Coast Railroad, 57
Florida Power & Light, 53
Ford Administration, 61
Ford Motor Credit, 85
Foreign bonds:
   fixed-charge coverage of, 102, 104
   how ratings differ from domestic
     debt ratings, 102-103, 104
   indentures of, 100-101, 104
   see also Foreign companies; *and*
     Foreign governments
Foreign companies, 99, 105
   asset protection of, 101
   earning power of, 101-102, 103
   financial resources of, 101, 102
   French petroleum firms, 104
   information required of, 100, 105
   Japanese firms, 102
   management of, 100, 102, 103
   special rating criteria for, 100
   see also Foreign bonds
Foreign governments, 99
   accounting methods of, 104
   communist, 103
   economies of, 105, 106
   information required of, 105
   international economic relations of,
     106
   management of, 105
   political structures of, 103, 105, 106
   see also Foreign bonds; *and listings*
     of individual countries
Fortune, 110

Fort Worth, Texas, 122
France, 104
Franklin National Bank, 76
Fruehauf Finance, 85

General Electric Credit, 86, 87
General Foods, 41
General Motors Acceptance Corporation, 16, 85
General obligation bonds, 135
   definition of, 17, 115
   fixed-charge coverage of, 122, 123
   indentures of, 117
   see also General obligation bond
     issuers
General obligation bond issuers:
   administrative factors, 117, 118-120
   current financial account analysis,
     117, 120-122
   debt factors, 117-118, 122
   economic factors, 117, 120, 122
   information required of, 115-117
   see also General obligation bonds;
     and Schools
Gould, Juliette L., ix, 24, 111, 112, 113-114, 141
Grand Prairie, Texas, 122, 123
Grossman, Hyman C., ix, 120, 121, 126, 142, 143

Harries, Brenton W., viii, 6, 16, 102
Haugen, Signe, ix
Henry Ford Hospital, 135
Homestead, Florida, 128, 129
Hospital bonds:
   fixed-charge coverage of, 134
   indentures of, 130
   see also Hospitals
Hospital consulting firms, 130, 131, 132
Hospitals:
   earning power of, 133-134
   information required of, 130-131
   management of, 132, 134
   medical staffs of, 132
   see also Hospital bonds and listings
     for specific hospitals
Housing Act of 1937, 129-130
Housing bonds, 129-130

Housing and Urban Development Department, U.S., 129, 130
Huff, Richard E., ix, 121, 125, 130, 131, 132, 133, 134, 142

ICI North America, 103
Imperial Chemical Industries Ltd., 103
Indentures:
 definition of, 28
 see also listings for various kinds of bonds, e.g., Utility bonds
Industrial bonds:
 definition of, 27
 fixed-charge coverage of, 35, 37
 indentures of, 28, 29
 see also Industrial companies
Industrial companies:
 asset protection of, 28, 29-31
 earning power of, 33-35
 financial resources of, 32-33
 information required of, 27-28
 management of, 35-36
 see also Industrial bonds; *and listings for specific companies*
Industries:
 canning, 112
 copper, 29n
 gas, 29n, 59, 61
 oil, 29n, 59, 106
 publishing, 36
 shipping, 56
 steel, 32
 trucking, 55, 56, 59
 see also listings for individual companies
Inflation, 2, 5
 impact on insurance companies, 94, 95
 revenue projects, 126
 utilities, 47, 50
Insurance bonds:
 fixed-charge coverage of, 90, 97
 indentures of, 91
 see also Insurance companies
Insurance companies:
 assets of, 91-94, 97, 98
 fire and casualty, 89, 90, 93, 94, 95, 96, 97
 information required of, 90-91
 liabilities of, 94-96
 life, 43, 90, 92, 93, 94, 95, 96, 97
 management of, 91, 97
 subsidiaries of, 89, 91, 97-98
 see also Insurance bonds; *and listings for individual companies*
Interest:
 bank sensitivity to, 68, 69, 76, 83
 on bonds, 23, 107
  commercial paper, 14, 109
  private placements, 43
 impact on finance companies, 80
  insurance companies, 135
 increases in, 2-3, 40
Intermediate-term bonds, 39-41
International Monetary Fund, 105
Interstate Commerce Commission, 56, 60
Irving Trust Company, 145
Italy, 103

Japan, 102, 104
Johnston, Norman, ix, 65, 66, 67, 74, 75, 76, 77

Kansas City, Missouri, 78
Kaufman, Henry, 2, 5, 12
Kennedy, Edward M., 62

Leases, 44-45
 amount of, 32, 49
 capitalization of, 31-32, 49-50, 63
Leverage:
 definition of, 49
 double, 74-75
Los Angeles Department of Water & Power, 128

McGraw-Hill Inc., v, vi
Management:
 advice to, 138-143
 see also listings for various kinds of companies
Margolies, Robert L., ix, 25
Massachusetts General Hospital, 135
Missouri, 78
Money markets, 67, 68
Moody's Investor Service, Inc., v
Moral obligation bonds, 3-4, 127-128
Morgan Guaranty Trust, 77
Morgan, J. P. & Co., 77

Index

Mortgages, 29, 45, 56, 92, 101, 131
Mortgage bonds, definition of, 48
Moser, Donald A., ix
Municipalities (states and cities):
   faults of issuers, vii, 4, 118, 119, 121-122, 143
   pension liabilities of, 119
   see also General obligation bonds; Revenue bonds; Revenue bond issuers; *and* Schools

National Accident & Life Insurance Co., 98
National Municipal League, 122
NCR, 19
New Jersey Turnpike Authority, 125
New York City, 67, 138, 145
   financial crisis of, vii, 4, 118, 119, 121-122
New York State:
   financial crisis of, vii
   moral obligation bonds of, 3-4
New York Times, The, 3
NLT Corp., 98
North Carolina, 143
Notes:
   corporate, 39, 41, 45
   definition of, 41
   municipal, 25

Off-balance sheet financing, *see* Leases
Ohio, 48
O'Meara, James J., ix, 91, 93, 97, 98
O'Neill, Leo C., ix, 6, 13, 15, 33, 35, 36
Outlook, The, vi

Pan American, 62
Parking systems, 124
Peck, Jane S., ix
Pennsylvania, 119
Pennsylvania Company, 9
Penn Central Railroad, 9
Pfeiffer, John K., ix, 119, 120, 143
Philadelphia, 122
Poland, 103
Pollution-control bonds, 44
Private placements, 21n, 39, 138
   and insurance companies, 89, 92
   bank, 65, 66
   leases, 44-45
   municipal, 25
Property:
   accounts, 31
   funds, 48
   personal, 44, 45
   personality, 116
   valuation of, 116, 117, 120
   see also Real estate

Railroad bonds:
   fixed-charge coverage of, 55, 56, 57
   indentures of, 56, 57-58
   see also Railroad companies
Railroad companies:
   asset protection of, 58
   earning power of, 55, 56, 59-60, 61
   financial resources of, 58-59
   information required of, 56
   management of, 60-61
   see also Railroad bonds; *and listings for specific railroads*
Ratings:
   appeals of, 22, 24, 26, 66, 107, 110, 137, 141
   complexity of, vii, viii, 6
   definitions of, 10-12, 13-19, 28
   impact of, vi, 9-10
   preliminary, 23, 26, 66n, 138, 141
   private placements, 43-44
   publication of, 21, 25, 107, 110, 138
   purpose of, 6
   quality of corporate, 12, 47
   of municipal, 12
   reviews of, 13, 22, 24, 26, 54, 141-142
   withdrawal of, 143
Rating of Corporate Debt Issues, The, 145
Ratios, financial:
   importance of, viii, 30, 35, 49, 58, 60, 97, 137
   see also Fixed-charge coverage
Real estate, 44, 45, 116
   subsidiaries, 59, 89, 97, 98
   see also Property
Real estate investment trusts, vii
Regulation:
   of airlines, 62, 64

of commercial banks, 75
of finance companies, 80
of insurance companies, 90, 93, 96, 98
of railroads, 56, 60, 61
of utilities, 47, 50-51, 52, 53, 54, 126, 128, 129
Revenue bonds:
  definition of, 17, 115
  fixed-charge coverage of, 125, 129
  indentures of, 123, 125, 126, 127, 128
  see also Municipalities *and* Revenue bond issuers
Revenue bond issuers:
  debt service coverage of, 123, 125, 126, 129
  information required of, 123-124
  management of, 125, 127
  revenues of, 123-124, 125, 126, 128, 129
  see also Municipalities; Hospitals; *and* Revenue bonds
Revenue sharing, 121, 123
Richmond, Virginia, 4
Rush-Presbyterian Hospital, 132

St. Louis, Missouri, 78
Salomon Brothers, 2, 12, 27, 47, 55
Schools, 116, 120, 121, 142
Sears, Roebuck, 16, 80
Securities Exchange Act of 1934, 115
Securities & Exchange Commission, 22, 27, 43, 99, 104, 109, 115, 138, 142
Seaman, Michael J., ix
Sewerage systems, 116, 122, 124
Shell Oil, 16
Sinking funds, reasons for, 29
Standard & Poor's Corp.:
  analysts, attitudes of, 22-26, 137, 140, 142
  criticism of, viii
  importance of, v
  operations of corporate finance department, 21-24
    of municipal finance department, 24-26
Stock:
  fixed-charge coverage of
    preferred, 42
  markets, 65, 66
  preferred, 39, 42-43, 65, 67, 92
Subsidiaries, 28, 139
  bank, 67, 68, 74, 75, 77
  finance company, 80, 85, 86
  foreign, 103
  insurance company, 89, 91, 97, 98
  railroad company, 59, 61

Taxes:
  ad valorem, 122
  capital gains, 93
  collection of, 116, 119-120, 123
  credits, 34, 51
  deferred, 58
  interest equalization, 99
  personal income, 118-119, 120
  property, 117, 118-120
  rates, 116, 119
  sales, 118-119
10-K reports, 22, 27, 66
10-Q reports, 22
Tennessee Valley Authority, 13
Treasury Department, U.S., 13, 14, 109

Union Carbide, 16
United Airlines, 63
U.S. Congress, 115
U.S. Government, 99
  deficit financing by, 2
  guarantees by, 56, 129, 130
  monetary policy of, 5
  see also listings of various departments and agencies
United States Steel, 37
Utah, 122
Utah, University of, 122
Utility bonds:
  fixed-charge coverage of, 48, 52, 53, 54
  indentures of, 48
  see also Utility companies
Utility companies:
  asset protection of, 47-49
  earning power of, 50-52
  financial resources of, 50
  information required of, *see same listing for* Industrial bonds

Index

   management of, 51-53, 54
   see also Utility bonds

Valuation reserve, bank, 68, 71n, 77
Veterans Administration, 92
Virginia, 53
VSI Corp., 114

Water-supply and -treatment systems, 124, 126, 128, 129

Weinberger, Roy P., ix, 6, 34, 50, 51, 52, 102, 103, 138, 139, 140, 142
Westinghouse Credit, 86
West Virginia, 53
Working capital, 49
   definition of, 31
   importance of, 32, 101, 134
World War II, 103

Xerox, 40

COALINGA STACKS
203872
332.67 SHE
How corporate and municipal debt i

203872

332.67
SHE   Sherwood, Hugh C.

          How corporate and
          municipal debt is
          rated

DATE DUE

DEC 3 '7?			
12-1-06			

WEST HILLS COLLEGE LIBRARY
COALINGA, CALIFORNIA